A Year in the Fields

by John Burroughs

CONTENTS

JOHN BURROUGHS A BIOGRAPHICAL SKETCH

BY CLIFTON JOHNSON

In the town of Roxbury, among the western Catskills, was born April 3, 1837, John Burroughs. The house in which he first saw the light was an unpainted, squarish structure, only a single story high, with a big chimney in the middle. This house was removed a few years later, and a better and somewhat larger one, which still stands, was built in its place. The situation is very pleasing. Roundabout is a varied country of heights, dales, woods and pastures, and cultivated fields. The dwelling is in a wide upland hollow that falls away to the east and south into a deep valley, beyond which rise line on line of great mounding hills. These turn blue in the distance and look like immense billows rolling in from a distant ocean.

There were nine children in the Burroughs family, and John was one of the younger members of this numerous household. He was a true country boy, acquainted with all the hard work and all the pleasures of an old-fashioned farm life. His people were poor and he had his own way to make in the world, but the environment was on the whole a salutary one.

He has always had a marked affection for the place of his birth, and he rejoices in the fact that from an eminence near his present home on the Hudson he can see mountains that are visible from his native hills. Two or three times every year he goes back to these hills to renew his youth among the familiar scenes of his boyhood.

"Johnny" Burroughs, as he was known to his home folks and the neighbors, was very like the other youngsters of the region in his interests, his ways, and his work. Yet as compared with them he undoubtedly had a livelier imagination, and things made a keener impression on his mind. In some cases his sensitiveness was more disturbing than gratifying. When his grandfather told "spook" stories to the children gathered around the evening blaze of the kitchen fireplace, John's hair would almost stand on end and he was afraid of every shadow.

He went to school in the little red schoolhouse across the valley, and as he grew older he aspired to attend an academy. But he had to make the opportunity for himself, and only succeeded in doing so at the age of seventeen, when he raised the needful money by six months of teaching. This enabled him in the autumn of 1854 to enter the Heading Literary Institute at Ashland. He found the life there enjoyable, but his funds ran low by spring and he was obliged to return to the farm. Until September he labored among his native fields, then took up teaching again. When pay day came he set off for a seminary of some note at Cooperstown, where a single term brought his student days forever to a close, and after another period of farm work at home he borrowed a small sum of money and journeyed to Illinois. Near Freeport he secured a school at forty dollars a month, which was much more than he could have earned in the East. Yet he gave up his position at the end of six months. "I came back," he says, "because of 'the girl I left behind me'; and it was pretty hard to stay even as long as I did."

Soon afterward he married. His total capital at the time was fifty dollars, a sum which was reduced one fifth by the wedding expenses. For several years he continued to teach, and at the age of twenty-five we find him in charge of a school near West Point. Up to this time his interest in nature and his aptitude for observation lay dormant. But now it was awakened by reading a volume of Audubon which chanced to fall into his hands. That was a revelation, and he went to the woods with entirely new interest and enthusiasm. He began at once to get acquainted with the birds, his vision grew keen and alert, and birds he had passed by before, he now saw at once.

Meanwhile the Civil War was going on, and it aroused in Burroughs a strong desire to enlist. He visited Washington to get a closer view of army life, but what he saw of it rather damped his military ardor. It seemed to him that the men were driven about and herded like cattle; and when a peaceful position in the Treasury Department was offered him he accepted it, and for nine years was a Government clerk.

At the Treasury he guarded a vault and kept a record of the money that went in or out. The duties were not arduous, and in his long intervals of leisure his mind wandered far afield. It dwelt on the charm of flitting wings and bird melodies, on the pleasures of rambling along country roads and into the woodlands; and, sitting before the Treasury vault, at a high desk and facing an iron wall he began to write. There was no need for notes. His memory was all-sufficient, and the result was the essays which make "Wake-Robin,"--his first book.

By 1873 Burroughs had had enough of the routine of a Government clerkship, and he resigned to become the receiver of a bank in Middletown, New York. Later he accepted a position as bank examiner in the eastern part of the State. But his longing to return to the soil was growing apace, and presently he bought a little farm on the west shore of the Hudson. He at once erected a substantial stone house and started orchards and vineyards, yet it was not until 1885 that he felt he could relinquish his Government position and dwell on his own land with the assurance of a safe support.

He has never been a great traveler. Still, he has been abroad twice and has recently made a trip to Alaska. Lesser excursions have taken him to Virginia and Kentucky, and to Canada, and he has camped in Maine and the Adirondacks. But the district that he knows best and that he puts oftenest into his nature studies is his home country in the Catskills and the region about his "Riverby" farm. Very little of his writing, however, has been done in the house in which he lives. This was never a wholly satisfactory working-place. He felt he must get away from all conventionalities, and he early put up on the outskirts of his vineyards a little bark-covered study, to which it has been his habit to retire for his indoor thinking and writing. He still uses this study more or less, and often in the summer evenings sits in an easy-chair, under an apple-tree just outside the door, and listens to the voices of Nature while he looks off across the Hudson.

But the spot that at present most engages his affection is a reclaimed woodland swamp, back among some rocky hills, a mile or two from the river. A few years ago the swamp was a wild tangle of brush and stumps, fallen trees and murky pools. Now it has been cleared and drained, and the dark forest mould produces wonderful crops of celery, sweet corn, potatoes, and other vegetables. On a shoulder of rock near the swamp borders Burroughs has built a rustic house, sheathed outside with slabs, and smacking in all its arrangements of the woodlands and of the days of pioneering. It has an open fireplace, where the flames crackle cheerfully on chilly evenings, and over the fireplace coals most of the cooking is done; but in really hot weather an oil stove serves instead.

On the other side of the hollow a delightfully cold spring bubbles forth, and immediately back of the house is a natural cavern which makes an ideal storage place for perishable foods. The descent to the cavern is made by a rude ladder, and the sight of Burroughs coming and going between it and the house has a most suggestive touch of the wild and romantic.

He is often at "Slabsides"--sometimes for weeks or months at a time, though he always makes daily visits to the valley to look after the work in his vineyards and to visit the post-office at the railway station. He is a leisurely man, to whom haste and the nervous pursuit of wealth or fame are totally foreign. He thoroughly enjoys country loitering, and when he gets a hint of anything interesting or new going on among the birds and little creatures of the fields, he likes to stop and investigate. His ears are remarkably quick and his eyes and sense of smell phenomenally acute, and much which to most of us would be unperceived or meaningless he reads as if it were an open book. Best of all, he has the power of imparting his enjoyment, and what he writes is full of outdoor fragrance, racy, piquant, and individual. His snap and vivacity are wholly unartificial. They are a part of the man--a man full of imagination and sensitiveness, a philosopher, a humorist, a hater of shams and pretension. The tenor of his life changes little from year to year, his affections remain steadfast, and this hardy, gray poet of things rural will continue, as ever, the warm-hearted nature enthusiast, and inspirer of the love of nature in others.

A YEAR IN THE FIELDS

I

A SNOW-STORM

That is a striking line with which Emerson opens his beautiful poem of the Snow-Storm:--

"Announced by all the trumpets of the sky, Arrives the snow, and, driving o'er the fields, Seems nowhere to alight."

One seems to see the clouds puffing their cheeks as they sound the charge of their white legions. But the line is more accurately descriptive of a rain-storm, as, in both summer and winter, rain is usually preceded by wind. Homer, describing a snow-storm in his time, says:--

"The winds are lulled."

The preparations of a snow-storm are, as a rule, gentle and quiet; a marked hush pervades both the earth and the sky. The movements of the celestial forces are muffled, as if the snow already paved the way of their coming. There is no uproar, no clashing of arms, no blowing of wind trumpets. These soft, feathery, exquisite crystals are formed as if in the silence and privacy of the inner cloud-chambers. Rude winds would break the spell and mar the process. The clouds are smoother, and slower in their movements, with less definite outlines than those which bring rain. In fact, everything is prophetic of the gentle and noiseless meteor that is approaching, and of the stillness that is to succeed it, when "all the batteries of sound are spiked," as Lowell says, and "we see the movements of life as a deaf man sees it,--a mere wraith of the clamorous existence that inflicts itself on our ears when the ground is bare." After the storm is fairly launched the winds not infrequently awake, and, seeing their opportunity, pipe the flakes a lively dance. I am speaking now of the typical, full-born midwinter storm that comes to us from the North or N. N. E., and that piles the landscape knee-deep with snow. Such a storm once came to us the last day of January,--the master-storm of the winter. Previous to that date, we had had but light snow. The spruces had been able to catch it all upon their arms, and keep a circle of bare ground beneath them where the birds scratched. But the day following this fall, they stood with their lower branches completely buried. If the Old Man of the North had but sent us his couriers and errand-boys before, the old graybeard appeared himself at our doors on this occasion, and we were all his subjects. His flag was upon every tree and roof, his seal upon every door and window, and his embargo upon every path and highway. He slipped down upon us, too, under the cover of such a bright, seraphic day,--a day that disarmed suspicion with all but the wise ones, a day without a cloud or a film, a gentle breeze from the west, a dry, bracing air, a blazing sun that brought out the bare ground under the lee of the fences and farm-buildings, and at night a spotless moon near her full. The next morning the sky reddened in the east, then became gray, heavy, and silent. A seamless cloud covered it. The smoke from the chimneys went up with a barely perceptible slant toward the north. In the forenoon the cedar-birds, purple finches, yellowbirds, nuthatches, bluebirds, were in flocks or in couples and trios about the trees, more or less noisy and loquacious. About noon a thin white veil began to blur the distant southern mountains. It was like a white dream slowly descending upon them. The first flake or flakelet that reached me was a mere white speck that came idly circling and eddying to the ground. I could not see it after it alighted. It might have been a scale from the feather of some passing bird, or a larger mote in the air that the stillness was allowing to settle. Yet it was the altogether inaudible and infinitesimal trumpeter that announced the coming storm, the grain of sand that heralded the desert. Presently another fell, then another; the white mist was creeping up the river valley. How slowly and loiteringly it came, and how microscopic its first siftings!

This mill is bolting its flour very fine, you think. But wait a little; it gets coarser by and by; you begin to see the flakes; they increase in numbers and in size, and before one o'clock it is snowing steadily. The flakes come straight down, but in a half hour they have a marked slant toward the north; the wind is taking a hand in the game. By mid-afternoon the storm is coming in regular pulse-beats or in vertical waves. The wind is not strong, but seems steady; the pines hum, yet there is a sort of rhythmic throb in the meteor; the air toward the wind looks ribbed with steady-moving vertical waves of snow. The impulses travel along like undulations in a vast suspended white curtain, imparted by some invisible hand there in the northeast. As the day declines the storm waxes, the wind increases, the snow-fall thickens, and "the housemates sit Around the radiant fireplace, inclosed In a tumultuous privacy of storm,"

a privacy which you feel outside as well as in. Out-of-doors you seem in a vast tent of snow; the distance is shut out, near-by objects are hidden; there are white curtains above you and white screens about you, and you feel housed and secluded in storm. Your friend leaves your door, and he is wrapped away in white obscurity, caught up in a cloud, and his footsteps are obliterated. Travelers meet on the road, and do not see or hear each other till they are face to face. The passing train, half a mile away, gives forth a mere wraith of sound. Its whistle is deadened as in a dense wood.

Still the storm rose. At five o'clock I went forth to face it in a two-mile walk. It was exhilarating in the extreme. The snow was lighter than chaff. It had been dried in the Arctic ovens to the last degree. The foot sped through it without hindrance. I fancied the grouse and the quail quietly sitting down in the open places, and letting it drift over them. With head under wing, and wing snugly folded, they would be softly and tenderly buried in a few moments. The mice and the squirrels were in their dens, but I fancied the fox asleep upon some rock or log, and allowing the flakes to cover him. The hare in her form, too, was being warmly sepulchred with the rest. I thought of the young cattle and the sheep huddled together on the lee side of a haystack in some remote field, all enveloped in mantles of white.

"I thought me on the ourie cattle, Or silly sheep, wha bide this brattle O' wintry war, Or thro' the drift, deep-lairing sprattle, Beneath a scaur.

"Ilk happing bird, wee helpless thing, That in the merry months o' spring Delighted me to hear thee sing, What comes o' thee? Where wilt thou cow'r thy chittering wing, And close thy ee?"

As I passed the creek, I noticed the white woolly masses that filled the water. It was as if somebody upstream had been washing his sheep and the water had carried away all the wool, and I thought of the Psalmist's phrase, "He giveth snow like wool." On the river a heavy fall of snow simulates a thin layer of cotton batting. The tide drifts it along, and, where it meets with an obstruction alongshore, it folds up and becomes wrinkled or convoluted like a fabric, or like cotton sheeting. Attempt to row a boat through it, and it seems indeed like cotton or wool, every fibre of which resists your progress.

As the sun went down and darkness fell, the storm impulse reached its full. It became a wild conflagration of wind and snow; the world was wrapt in frost flame; it enveloped one, and penetrated his lungs and caught away his breath like a blast from a burning city. How it whipped around and under every cover and searched out every crack and crevice, sifting under the shingles in the attic, darting its white tongue under the kitchen door, puffing its breath down the chimney, roaring through the woods, stalking like a sheeted ghost across the hills, bending in white and ever-changing forms above the fences, sweeping across the plains, whirling in eddies behind the buildings, or leaping spitefully up their walls,--in short, taking the world entirely to itself, and giving a loose rein to its desire.

But in the morning, behold! the world was not consumed; it was not the besom of destruction, after all, but the gentle hand of mercy. How deeply and warmly and spotlessly Earth's nakedness is clothed!--the "wool" of the Psalmist nearly two feet deep. And as far as warmth and protection are concerned, there is a good deal of the virtue of wool in such a snow-fall. How it protects the grass, the plants, the roots of the trees, and the worms, insects, and smaller animals in the ground! It is a veritable fleece, beneath which the shivering earth ("the frozen hills ached with pain," says one of our young poets) is restored to warmth. When the temperature of the air is at zero, the thermometer, placed at the surface of the ground beneath a foot and a half of snow, would probably indicate but a few degrees below freezing; the snow is rendered such a perfect non-conductor of heat mainly by reason of the quantity of air that is caught and retained between the crystals. Then how, like a fleece of wool, it rounds and fills out the landscape, and makes the leanest and most angular field look smooth!

The day dawned, and continued as innocent and fair as the day which had preceded,--two mountain peaks of sky and sun, with their valley of cloud and snow between. Walk to the nearest spring run on such a morning, and you can see the Colorado valley and the great cañons of the West in miniature, carved in alabaster. In the midst of the plain of snow lie these chasms; the vertical walls, the bold headlands, the turrets and spires and obelisks, the rounded and towering capes, the carved and buttressed precipices, the branch valleys and cañons, and the winding and tortuous course of the main channel are all here,--all that the Yosemite or Yellowstone have to show, except the terraces and the cascades. Sometimes my cañon is bridged, and one's fancy runs nimbly across a vast arch of Parian marble, and that makes up for the falls and the terraces. Where the ground is marshy, I come upon a pretty and vivid illustration of what I have read and been told of the Florida formation. This white and brittle limestone is undermined by water. Here are the dimples and depressions, the sinks and the wells, the springs and the lakes. Some places a mouse might break through the surface and reveal the water far beneath, or the snow gives way of its own weight, and you have a minute Florida well, with the truncated cone-shape and all. The arched and subterranean pools and passages are there likewise.

But there is a more beautiful and fundamental geology than this in the snow-storm: we are admitted into Nature's oldest laboratory, and see the working of the law by which the foundations of the material universe were laid,--the law or mystery of crystallization. The earth is built upon crystals; the granite rock is only a denser and more compact snow, or a kind of ice that was vapor once and may be vapor again. "Every stone is nothing else but a congealed lump of frozen earth," says Plutarch. By cold and pressure air can be liquefied, perhaps solidified. A little more time, a little more heat, and the hills are but April snow-banks. Nature has but two forms, the cell and the crystal,--the crystal first, the cell last. All organic nature is built up of the cell; all inorganic, of the crystal. Cell upon cell rises the vegetable, rises the animal; crystal wedded to and compacted with crystal stretches the earth beneath them. See in the falling snow the old cooling and precipitation, and the shooting, radiating forms that are the architects of planet and globe.

We love the sight of the brown and ruddy earth; it is the color of life, while a snow-covered plain is the face of death; yet snow is but the mask of the life-giving rain; it, too, is the friend of man,--the tender, sculpturesque, immaculate, warming, fertilizing snow.

II

WINTER NEIGHBORS

The country is more of a wilderness, more of a wild solitude, in the winter than in the summer. The wild comes out. The urban, the cultivated, is hidden or negatived. You shall hardly know a good field from a poor, a meadow from a pasture, a park from a forest. Lines and boundaries are disregarded; gates and bar-ways are unclosed; man lets go his hold upon the earth; title-deeds are deep buried beneath the snow; the best-kept grounds relapse to a state of nature; under the pressure of the cold, all the wild creatures become outlaws, and roam abroad beyond their usual haunts. The partridge comes to the orchard for buds; the rabbit comes to the garden and lawn; the crows and jays come to the ash-heap and corn-crib, the snow buntings to the stack and to the barnyard; the sparrows pilfer from the domestic fowls; the pine grosbeak comes down from the north and shears your maples of their buds; the fox prowls about your premises at night; and the red squirrels find your grain in the barn or steal the butternuts from your attic. In fact, winter, like some great calamity, changes the status of most creatures and sets them adrift. Winter, like poverty, makes us acquainted with strange bedfellows.

For my part, my nearest approach to a strange bedfellow is the little gray rabbit that has taken up her abode under my study floor. As she spends the day here and is out larking at night, she is not much of a bedfellow, after all. It is probable that I disturb her slumbers more than she does mine. I think she is some support to me under there,--a silent, wide-eyed witness and backer; a type of the gentle and harmless in savage nature. She has no sagacity to give me or lend me, but that soft, nimble foot of hers, and that touch as of cotton wherever she goes, are worthy of emulation. I think I can feel her goodwill through the floor, and I hope she can mine. When I have a happy thought, I imagine her ears twitch, especially when I think of the sweet apple I will place by her doorway at night. I wonder if that fox chanced to catch a glimpse of her the other night when he stealthily leaped over the fence near by and walked along between the study and the house? How clearly one could read that it was not a little dog that had passed there! There was something furtive in the track; it shied off away from the house and around it, as if eying it suspiciously; and then it had the caution and deliberation of the fox,--bold, bold, but not too bold; wariness was in every footprint. If it had been a little dog that had chanced to wander that way, when he crossed my path he would have followed it up to the barn and have gone smelling around for a bone; but this sharp, cautious track held straight across all others, keeping five or six rods from the house, up the hill, across the highway toward a neighboring farmstead, with its nose in the air, and its eye and ear alert, so to speak.

A winter neighbor of mine, in whom I am interested, and who perhaps lends me his support after his kind, is a little red owl, whose retreat is in the heart of an old apple-tree just over the fence. Where he keeps himself in spring and summer, I do not know, but late every fall, and at intervals all winter, his hiding-place is discovered by the jays and nuthatches, and proclaimed from the treetops for the space of half an hour or so, with all the powers of voice they can command. Four times during one winter they called me out to behold this little ogre feigning sleep in his den, sometimes in one apple-tree, sometimes in another. Whenever I heard their cries, I knew my neighbor was being berated. The birds would take turns at looking in upon him, and uttering their alarm-notes. Every jay within hearing would come to the spot, and at once approach the hole in the trunk or limb, and with a kind of breathless eagerness and excitement take a peep at the owl, and then join the outcry. When I approached they would hastily take a final look, and then withdraw and regard my movements intently. After accustoming my eye to the faint light of the cavity for a few moments, I could usually make out the owl at the bottom feigning sleep. Feigning, I say, because this is what he really did, as I first discovered one day when I cut into his retreat with the axe. The loud blows and the falling chips did not disturb him at all. When I reached in a stick and pulled him over on his side, leaving one of his wings spread out, he made no attempt to recover himself, but lay among the chips and fragments of decayed wood, like a part of themselves. Indeed, it took a sharp eye to distinguish him. Not till I had pulled him forth by one wing, rather rudely, did he abandon his trick of simulated sleep or death. Then, like a detected pickpocket, he was suddenly transformed into another creature. His eyes flew wide open, his talons clutched my finger, his ears were depressed, and every motion and look said, "Hands off, at your peril." Finding this game did not work, he soon began to "play 'possum" again. I put a cover over my study wood-box and kept him captive for a week. Look in upon him at any time, night or day, and he was apparently wrapped in the profoundest slumber; but the live mice which I put into his box from time to time found his sleep was easily broken; there would be a sudden rustle in the box, a faint squeak, and then silence. After a week of captivity I gave him his freedom in the full sunshine: no trouble for him to see which way and where to go.

Just at dusk in the winter nights, I often hear his soft bur-r-r-r, very pleasing and bell-like. What a furtive, woody sound it is in the winter stillness, so unlike the harsh scream of the hawk! But all the ways of the owl are ways of softness and duskiness. His wings are shod with silence, his plumage is edged with down.

Another owl neighbor of mine, with whom I pass the time of day more frequently than with the last, lives farther away. I pass his castle every night on my way to the post-office, and in winter, if the hour is late enough, am pretty sure to see him standing in his doorway, surveying the passers-by and the landscape through narrow slits in his eyes. For four successive winters now have I observed him. As the twilight begins to deepen, he rises up out of his cavity in the apple-tree, scarcely faster than the moon rises from behind the hill, and sits in the opening, completely framed by its outlines of gray bark and dead wood, and by his protective coloring virtually invisible to every eye that does not know he is there. Probably my own is the only eye that has ever penetrated his secret, and mine never would have done so had I not chanced on one occasion to see him leave his retreat and make a raid upon a shrike that was impaling a shrew-mouse upon a thorn in a neighboring tree, and which I was watching. Failing to get the mouse, the owl returned swiftly to his cavity, and ever since, while going that way, I have been on the lookout for him. Dozens of teams and foot-passengers pass him late in the day, but he regards them not, nor they him. When I come along and pause to salute him, he opens his eyes a little wider, and, appearing to recognize me, quickly shrinks and fades into the background of his door in a very weird and curious manner. When he is not at his outlook, or when he is, it requires the best powers of the eye to decide the point, as the empty cavity itself is almost an exact image of him. If the whole thing had been carefully studied, it could not have answered its purpose better. The owl stands quite perpendicular, presenting a front of light mottled gray; the eyes are closed to a mere slit, the ear-feathers depressed, the beak buried in the plumage, and the whole attitude is one of silent, motionless waiting and observation. If a mouse should be seen crossing the highway, or scudding over any exposed part of the snowy surface in the twilight, the owl would doubtless swoop down upon it. I think the owl has learned to distinguish me from the rest of the passers-by; at least, when I stop before him, and he sees himself observed, he backs down into his den, as I have said, in a very amusing manner. Whether bluebirds, nuthatches, and chickadees--birds that pass the night in cavities of trees--ever run into the clutches of the dozing owl, I should be glad to know. My impression is, however, that they seek out smaller cavities. An old willow by the roadside blew down one summer, and a decayed branch broke open, revealing a brood of half-fledged owls, and many feathers and quills of bluebirds, orioles, and other songsters, showing plainly enough why all birds fear and berate the owl.

The English house sparrows, which are so rapidly increasing among us, and which must add greatly to the food supply of the owls and other birds of prey, seek to baffle their enemies by roosting in the densest evergreens they can find, in the arbor-vit? and in hemlock hedges. Soft-winged as the owl is, he cannot steal in upon such a retreat without giving them warning.

These sparrows are becoming about the most noticeable of my winter neighbors, and a troop of them every morning watch me put out the hens' feed, and soon claim their share. I rather encouraged them in their neighborliness, till one day I discovered the snow under a favorite plum-tree where they most frequently perched covered with the scales of the fruit-buds. On investigating, I found that the tree had been nearly stripped of its buds,--a very unneighborly act on the part of the sparrows, considering, too, all the cracked corn I had scattered for them. So I at once served notice on them that our good understanding was at an end. And a hint is as good as a kick with this bird. The stone I hurled among them, and the one with which I followed them up, may have been taken as a kick; but they were only a hint of the shot-gun that stood ready in the corner. The sparrows left in high dudgeon, and were not back again in some days, and were then very shy. No doubt the time is near at hand when we shall have to wage serious war upon these sparrows, as they long have had to do on the continent of Europe. And yet it will be hard to kill the little wretches, the only Old World bird we have. When I take down my gun to shoot them I shall probably remember that the Psalmist said, "I watch, and am as a sparrow alone upon the housetop," and maybe the recollection will cause me to stay my hand. The sparrows have the Old World hardiness and prolificness; they are wise and tenacious of life, and we shall find it by and by no small matter to keep them in check. Our native birds are much different, less prolific, less shrewd, less aggressive and persistent, less quick-witted and able to read the note of danger or hostility,--in short, less sophisticated. Most of our birds are yet essentially wild, that is, little changed by civilization. In winter, especially, they sweep by me and around me in flocks,-- the Canada sparrow, the snow bunting, the shore lark, the pine grosbeak, the redpoll, the cedar-bird,--feeding upon frozen apples in the orchard, upon cedar-berries, upon maple-buds, and the berries of the mountain-ash, and the celtis, and upon the seeds of the weeds that rise above the snow in the field, or upon the hayseed dropped where the cattle have been foddered in the barnyard or about the distant stack; but yet taking no heed of man, in no way changing their habits so as to take advantage of his presence in nature. The pine grosbeaks will come in numbers upon your porch to get the black drupes of the honeysuckle or the woodbine, or within reach of your windows to get the berries of the mountain-ash, but they know you not; they look at you as innocently and unconcernedly as at a bear or moose in their native north, and your house is no more to them than a ledge of rocks.

The only ones of my winter neighbors that actually rap at my door are the nuthatches and woodpeckers, and these do not know that it is my door. My retreat is covered with the bark of young chestnut-trees, and the birds, I suspect, mistake it for a huge stump that ought to hold fat grubs (there is not even a book-worm inside of it), and their loud rapping often makes me think I have a caller indeed. I place fragments of hickory-nuts in the interstices of the bark, and thus attract the nuthatches; a bone upon my window-sill attracts both nuthatches and the downy woodpecker. They peep in curiously through the window upon me, pecking away at my bone, too often a very poor one. A bone nailed to a tree a few feet in front of the window attracts crows as well as lesser birds. Even the slate-colored snowbird, a seed-eater, comes and nibbles it occasionally.

The bird that seems to consider he has the best right to the bone both upon the tree and upon the sill is the downy woodpecker, my favorite neighbor among the winter birds, to whom I will mainly devote the remainder of this chapter. His retreat is but a few paces from my own, in the decayed limb of an apple-tree which he excavated several autumns ago. I say "he" because the red plume on the top of his head proclaims the sex. It seems not to be generally known to our writers upon ornithology that certain of our woodpeckers--probably all the winter residents-- each fall excavate a limb or the trunk of a tree in which to pass the winter, and that the cavity is abandoned in the spring, probably for a new one in which nidification takes place. So far as I have observed, these cavities are drilled out only by the males. Where the females take up their quarters I am not so well informed, though I suspect that they use the abandoned holes of the males of the previous year.

The particular woodpecker to which I refer drilled his first hole in my apple-tree one fall four or five years ago. This he occupied till the following spring, when he abandoned it. The next fall he began a hole in an adjoining limb, later than before, and when it was about half completed a female took possession of his old quarters. I am sorry to say that this seemed to enrage the male very much, and he persecuted the poor bird whenever she appeared upon the scene. He would fly at her spitefully and drive her off. One chilly November morning, as I passed under the tree, I heard the hammer of the little architect in his cavity, and at the same time saw the persecuted female sitting at the entrance of the other hole as if she would fain come out. She was actually shivering, probably from both fear and cold. I understood the situation at a glance; the bird was afraid to come forth and brave the anger of the male. Not till I had rapped smartly upon the limb with my stick did she come out and attempt to escape; but she had not gone ten feet from the tree before the male was in hot pursuit, and in a few moments had driven her back to the same tree, where she tried to avoid him among the branches. A few days after, he rid himself of his unwelcome neighbor in the following ingenious manner: he fairly scuttled the other cavity; he drilled a hole into the bottom of it that let in the light and the cold, and I saw the female there no more. I did not see him in the act of rendering this tenement uninhabitable; but one morning, behold it was punctured at the bottom, and the circumstances all seemed to point to him as the author of it. There is probably no gallantry among the birds except at the mating season. I have frequently seen the male woodpecker drive the female away from the bone upon the tree. When she hopped around to the other end and timidly nibbled it, he would presently dart spitefully at her. She would then take up her position in his rear and wait till he had finished his meal. The position of the female among the birds is very much the same as that of woman among savage tribes. Most of the drudgery of life falls upon her, and the leavings of the males are often her lot.

My bird is a genuine little savage, doubtless, but I value him as a neighbor. It is a satisfaction during the cold or stormy winter nights to know he is warm and cosy there in his retreat. When the day is bad and unfit to be abroad in, he is there too. When I wish to know if he is at home, I go and rap upon his tree, and, if he is not too lazy or indifferent, after some delay he shows his head in his round doorway about ten feet above, and looks down inquiringly upon me,-- sometimes latterly I think half resentfully, as much as to say, "I would thank you not to disturb me so often." After sundown, he will not put his head out any more when I call, but as I step away I can get a glimpse of him inside looking cold and reserved. He is a late riser, especially if it is a cold or disagreeable morning, in this respect being like the barn fowls; it is sometimes near nine o'clock before I see him leave his tree. On the other hand, he comes home early, being in, if the day is unpleasant, by four P. M. He lives all alone; in this respect I do not commend his example. Where his mate is, I should like to know.

I have discovered several other woodpeckers in adjoining orchards, each of which has a like home, and leads a like solitary life. One of them has excavated a dry limb within easy reach of my hand, doing the work also in September. But the choice of tree was not a good one; the limb was too much decayed, and the workman had made the cavity too large; a chip had come out, making a hole in the outer wall. Then he went a few inches down the limb and began again, and excavated a large, commodious chamber, but had again come too near the surface; scarcely more than the bark protected him in one place, and the limb was very much weakened. Then he made another attempt still farther down the limb, and drilled in an inch or two, but seemed to change his mind; the work stopped, and I concluded the bird had wisely abandoned the tree. Passing there one cold, rainy November day, I thrust in my two fingers and was surprised to feel something soft and warm; as I drew away my hand the bird came out, apparently no more surprised than I was. It had decided, then, to make its home in the old limb; a decision it had occasion to regret, for not long after, on a stormy night, the branch gave way and fell to the ground:--

"When the bough breaks the cradle will fall, And down will come baby, cradle and all."

Such a cavity makes a snug, warm home, and when the entrance is on the under side of the limb, as is usual, the wind and snow cannot reach the occupant. Late in December, while crossing a high, wooded mountain, lured by the music of fox-hounds, I discovered fresh yellow chips strewing the new-fallen snow, and at once thought of my woodpeckers. On looking around I saw where one had been at work excavating a lodge in a small yellow birch. The orifice was about fifteen feet from the ground, and appeared as round as if struck with a compass. It was on the east side of the tree, so as to avoid the prevailing west and northwest winds. As it was nearly two inches in diameter, it could not have been the work of the downy, but must have been that of the hairy, or else the yellow-bellied woodpecker. His home had probably been wrecked by some violent wind, and he was thus providing himself another. In digging out these retreats the woodpeckers prefer a dry, brittle trunk, not too soft. They go in horizontally to the centre and then turn downward, enlarging the tunnel as they go, till when finished it is the shape of a long, deep pear.

Another trait our woodpeckers have that endears them to me, and that has never been pointedly noticed by our ornithologists, is their habit of drumming in the spring. They are songless birds, and yet all are musicians; thèy make the dry limbs eloquent of the coming change. Did you think that loud, sonorous hammering which proceeded from the orchard or from the near woods on that still March or April morning was only some bird getting its breakfast? It is downy, but he is not rapping at the door of a grub; he is rapping at the door of spring, and the dry limb thrills beneath the ardor of his blows. Or, later in the season, in the dense forest or by some remote mountain lake, does that measured rhythmic beat that breaks upon the silence, first three strokes following each other rapidly, succeeded by two louder ones with longer intervals between them, and that has an effect upon the alert ear as if the solitude itself had at last found a voice,--does that suggest anything less than a deliberate musical performance? In fact, our woodpeckers are just as characteristically drummers as is the ruffed grouse, and they have their particular limbs and stubs to which they resort for that purpose. Their need of expression is apparently just as great as that of the song-birds, and it is not surprising that they should have found out that there is music in a dry, seasoned limb which can be evoked beneath their beaks.

A few seasons ago, a downy woodpecker, probably the individual one who is now my winter neighbor, began to drum early in March in a partly decayed apple-tree that stands in the edge of a narrow strip of woodland near me. When the morning was still and mild I would often hear him through my window before I was up, or by half-past six o'clock, and he would keep it up pretty briskly till nine or ten o'clock, in this respect resembling the grouse, which do most of their drumming in the forenoon. His drum was the stub of a dry limb about the size of one's wrist. The heart was decayed and gone, but the outer shell was hard and resonant. The bird would keep his position there for an hour at a time. Between his drummings he would preen his plumage and listen as if for the response of the female, or for the drum of some rival. How swift his head would go when he was delivering his blows upon the limb! His beak wore the surface perceptibly. When he wished to change the key, which was quite often, he would shift his position an inch or two to a knot which gave out a higher, shriller note. When I climbed up to examine his drum he was much disturbed. I did not know he was in the vicinity, but it seems he saw me from a near tree, and came in haste to the neighboring branches, and with spread plumage and a sharp note demanded plainly enough what my business was with his drum. I was invading his privacy, desecrating his shrine, and the bird was much put out. After some weeks the female appeared; he had literally drummed up a mate; his urgent and oft-repeated advertisement was answered. Still the drumming did not cease, but was quite as fervent as before. If a mate could be won by drumming, she could be kept and entertained by more drumming; courtship should not end with marriage. If the bird felt musical before, of course he felt much more so now. Besides that, the gentle deities needed propitiating in behalf of the nest and young as well as in behalf of the mate. After a time a second female came, when there was war between the two. I did not see them come to blows, but I saw one female pursuing the other about the place, and giving her no rest for several days. She was evidently trying to run her out of the neighborhood. Now and then, she, too, would drum briefly, as if sending a triumphant message to her mate.

The woodpeckers do not each have a particular dry limb to which they resort at all times to drum, like the one I have described. The woods are full of suitable branches, and they drum more or less here and there as they are in quest of food; yet I am convinced each one has its favorite spot, like the grouse, to which it resorts especially in the morning. The sugar-maker in the maple-woods may notice that this sound proceeds from the same tree or trees about his camp with great regularity. A woodpecker in my vicinity has drummed for two seasons on a telegraph pole, and he makes the wires and glass insulators ring. Another drums on a thin board on the end of a long grape-arbor, and on still mornings can be heard a long distance.

A friend of mine in a Southern city tells me of a red-headed woodpecker that drums upon a lightning-rod on his neighbor's house. Nearly every clear, still morning at certain seasons, he says, this musical rapping may be heard. "He alternates his tapping with his stridulous call, and the effect on a cool, autumn-like morning is very pleasing."

The high-hole appears to drum more promiscuously than does downy. He utters his long, loud spring call, whick--whick--whick--whick, and then begins to rap with his beak upon his perch before the last note has reached your ear. I have seen him drum sitting upon the ridge of the barn. The log-cock, or pileated woodpecker, the largest and wildest of our Northern species, I have never heard drum. His blows should wake the echoes.

When the woodpecker is searching for food, or laying siege to some hidden grub, the sound of his hammer is dead or muffled, and is heard but a few yards. It is only upon dry, seasoned timber, freed of its bark, that he beats his reveille to spring and wooes his mate.

Wilson was evidently familiar with this vernal drumming of the woodpeckers, but quite misinterprets it. Speaking of the red-bellied species, he says: "It rattles like the rest of the tribe on the dead limbs, and with such violence as to be heard in still weather more than half a mile off; and listens to hear the insect it has alarmed." He listens rather to hear the drum of his rival, or the brief and coy response of the female; for there are no insects in these dry limbs.

On one occasion I saw downy at his drum when a female flew quickly through the tree and alighted a few yards beyond him. He paused instantly, and kept his place apparently without moving a muscle. The female, I took it, had answered his advertisement. She flitted about from limb to limb (the female may be known by the absence of the crimson spot on the back of the head), apparently full of business of her own, and now and then would drum in a shy, tentative manner. The male watched her a few moments, and, convinced perhaps that she meant business, struck up his liveliest tune, then listened for her response. As it came back timidly but promptly, he left his perch and sought a nearer acquaintance with the prudent female. Whether or not a match grew out of this little flirtation I cannot say.

Our smaller woodpeckers are sometimes accused of injuring the apple and other fruit trees, but the depredator is probably the larger and rarer yellow-bellied species. One autumn I caught one of these fellows in the act of sinking long rows of his little wells in the limb of an apple-tree. There were series of rings of them, one above another, quite around the stem, some of them the third of an inch across. They are evidently made to get at the tender, juicy bark, or cambium layer, next to the hard wood of the tree. The health and vitality of the branch are so seriously impaired by them that it often dies.

In the following winter the same bird (probably) tapped a maple-tree in front of my window in fifty-six places; and when the day was sunny, and the sap oozed out, he spent most of his time there. He knew the good sap-days, and was on hand promptly for his tipple; cold and cloudy days he did not appear. He knew which side of the tree to tap, too, and avoided the sunless northern exposure. When one series of well-holes failed to supply him, he would sink another, drilling through the bark with great ease and quickness. Then, when the day was warm, and the sap ran freely, he would have a regular sugar-maple debauch, sitting there by his wells hour after hour, and as fast as they became filled sipping out the sap. This he did in a gentle, caressing manner that was very suggestive. He made a row of wells near the foot of the tree, and other rows higher up, and he would hop up and down the trunk as these became filled. He would hop down the tree backward with the utmost ease, throwing his tail outward and his head inward at each hop. When the wells would freeze up or his thirst become slaked, he would ruffle his feathers, draw himself together, and sit and doze in the sun on the side of the tree. He passed the night in a hole in an apple-tree not far off. He was evidently a young bird, not yet having the plumage of the mature male or female, and yet he knew which tree to tap and where to tap it. I saw where he had bored several maples in the vicinity, but no oaks or chestnuts. I nailed up a fat bone near his sap-works: the downy woodpecker came there several times a day to dine; the nuthatch came, and even the snowbird took a taste occasionally; but this sapsucker never touched it--the sweet of the tree sufficed for him. This woodpecker does not breed or abound in my vicinity; only stray specimens are now and then to be met with in the colder months. As spring approached, the one I refer to took his departure.

I must bring my account of my neighbor in the tree down to the latest date; so after the lapse of a year I add the following notes. The last day of February was bright and spring-like. I heard the first sparrow sing that morning and the first screaming of the circling hawks, and about seven o'clock the first drumming of my little friend. His first notes were uncertain and at long intervals, but by and by he warmed up and beat a lively tattoo. As the season advanced he ceased to lodge in his old quarters. I would rap and find nobody at home. Was he out on a lark, I said, the spring fever working in his blood? After a time his drumming grew less frequent, and finally, in the middle of April, ceased entirely. Had some accident befallen him, or had he wandered away to fresh fields, following some siren of his species? Probably the latter. Another bird that I had under observation also left his winter-quarters in the spring. This, then, appears to be the usual custom. The wrens and the nuthatches and chickadees succeed to these abandoned cavities, and often have amusing disputes over them. The nuthatches frequently pass the night in them, and the wrens and chickadees nest in them. I have further observed that in excavating a cavity for a nest the downy woodpecker makes the entrance smaller than when he is excavating his winter-quarters. This is doubtless for the greater safety of the young birds.

The next fall the downy excavated another limb in the old apple-tree, but had not got his retreat quite finished when the large hairy woodpecker appeared upon the scene. I heard his loud click, click, early one frosty November morning. There was something impatient and angry in the tone that arrested my attention. I saw the bird fly to the tree where downy had been at work, and fall with great violence upon the entrance to his cavity. The bark and the chips flew beneath his vigorous blows, and, before I fairly woke up to what he was doing, he had completely demolished the neat, round doorway of downy. He had made a large, ragged opening, large enough for himself to enter. I drove him away and my favorite came back, but only to survey the ruins of his castle for a moment and then go away. He lingered about for a day or two and then disappeared. The big hairy usurper passed a night in the cavity; but on being hustled out of it the next night by me, he also left, but not till he had demolished the entrance to a cavity in a neighboring tree where downy and his mate had reared their brood that summer, and where I had hoped the female would pass the winter.

III

A SPRING RELISH

It is a little remarkable how regularly severe and mild winters alternate in our climate for a series of years,--a feminine and a masculine one, as it were, almost invariably following each other. Every other season now for ten years the ice-gatherers on the river have been disappointed of a full harvest, and every other season the ice has formed from fifteen to twenty inches thick. From 1873 to 1884 there was no marked exception to this rule. But in the last-named year, when, according to the succession, a mild winter was due, the breed seemed to have got crossed, and a sort of mongrel winter was the result; neither mild nor severe, but very stormy, capricious, and disagreeable, with ice a foot thick on the river. The winter which followed, that of 1884-85, though slow and hesitating at first, fully proved itself as belonging to the masculine order. The present winter of 1885-86 shows a marked return to the type of two years ago--less hail and snow, but by no means the mild season that was due. By and by, probably, the meteorological influences will get back into the old ruts again, and we shall have once more the regular alternation of mild and severe winters. During very open winters, like that of 1879-80, nature in my latitude, eighty miles north of New York, hardly shuts up house at all.

That season I heard a little piping frog on the 7th of December, and on the 18th of January, in a spring run, I saw the common bullfrog out of his hibernaculum, evidently thinking it was spring. A copperhead snake was killed here about the same date; caterpillars did not seem to retire, as they usually do, but came forth every warm day. The note of the bluebird was heard nearly every week all winter, and occasionally that of the robin. Such open winters make one fear that his appetite for spring will be blunted when spring really does come; but he usually finds that the April days have the old relish. April is that part of the season that never cloys upon the palate. It does not surfeit one with good things, but provokes and stimulates the curiosity. One is on the alert; there are hints and suggestions on every hand. Something has just passed, or stirred, or called, or breathed, in the open air or in the ground about, that we would fain know more of. May is sweet, but April is pungent. There is frost enough in it to make it sharp, and heat enough in it to make it quick.

In my walks in April, I am on the lookout for watercresses. It is a plant that has the pungent April flavor. In many parts of the country the watercress seems to have become completely naturalized, and is essentially a wild plant. I found it one day in a springy place, on the top of a high, wooded mountain, far from human habitation. We gathered it and ate it with our sandwiches. Where the walker cannot find this salad, a good substitute may be had in our native spring cress, which is also in perfection in April. Crossing a wooded hill in the regions of the Catskills on the 15th of the month, I found a purple variety of the plant, on the margin of a spring that issued from beneath a ledge of rocks, just ready to bloom. I gathered the little white tubers, that are clustered like miniature potatoes at the root, and ate them, and they were a surprise and a challenge to the tongue; on the table they would well fill the place of mustard, and horseradish, and other appetizers. When I was a schoolboy, we used to gather, in a piece of woods on our way to school, the roots of a closely allied species to eat with our lunch. But we generally ate it up before lunch-time. Our name for this plant was "Crinkle-root." The botanists call it the toothwort (Dentaria), also pepper-root.

From what fact or event shall one really date the beginning of spring? The little piping frogs usually furnish a good starting-point. One spring I heard the first note on the 6th of April; the next on the 27th of February; but in reality the latter season was only two weeks earlier than the former. When the bees carry in their first pollen, one would think spring had come; yet this fact does not always correspond with the real stage of the season. Before there is any bloom anywhere, bees will bring pollen to the hive. Where do they get it?

I have seen them gathering it on the fresh sawdust in the woodyard, especially on that of hickory or maple. They wallow amid the dust, working it over and over, and searching it like diamond-hunters, and after a time their baskets are filled with the precious flour, which is probably only a certain part of the wood, doubtless the soft, nutritious inner bark.

In fact, all signs and phases of life in the early season are very capricious, and are earlier or later just as some local or exceptional circumstance favors or hinders. It is only such birds as arrive after about the 20th of April that are at all "punctual" according to the almanac. I have never known the arrival of the barn swallow to vary much from that date in this latitude, no matter how early or late the season might be. Another punctual bird is the yellow redpoll warbler, the first of his class that appears. Year after year, between the 20th and the 25th, I am sure to see this little bird about my place for a day or two only, now on the ground, now on the fences, now on the small trees and shrubs, and closely examining the buds or just-opening leaves of the apple-trees. He is a small olive-colored bird, with a dark-red or maroon-colored patch on the top of his head. His ordinary note is a smart "chirp." His movements are very characteristic, especially that vertical, oscillating movement of the hind part of his body, like that of the wagtails. There are many birds that do not come here till May, be the season never so early. The spring of 1878 was very forward, and on the 27th of April I made this entry in my notebook: "In nature it is the middle of May, and, judging from vegetation alone, one would expect to find many of the later birds, as the oriole, the wood thrush, the kingbird, the catbird, the tanager, the indigo-bird, the vireos, and many of the warblers, but they have not arrived. The May birds, it seems, will not come in April, no matter how the season favors."

Some birds passing north in the spring are provokingly silent. Every April I see the hermit thrush hopping about the woods, and in case of a sudden snow-storm seeking shelter about the outbuildings; but I never hear even a fragment of his wild, silvery strain. The white-crowned sparrow also passes in silence. I see the bird for a few days about the same date each year, but he will not reveal to me his song. On the other hand, his congener, the white-throated sparrow, is decidedly musical in passing, both spring and fall. His sweet, wavering whistle is at times quite as full and perfect as when heard in June or July in the Canadian woods. The latter bird is much more numerous than the white-crowned, and its stay with us more protracted, which may in a measure account for the greater frequency of its song. The fox sparrow, who passes earlier (sometimes in March), is also chary of the music with which he is so richly endowed. It is not every season that I hear him, though my ear is on the alert for his strong, finely-modulated whistle.

Nearly all the warblers sing in passing. I hear them in the orchards, in the groves, in the woods, as they pause to feed in their northward journey, their brief, lisping, shuffling, insect-like notes requiring to be searched for by the ear, as their forms by the eye. But the ear is not tasked to identify the songs of the kinglets, as they tarry briefly with us in spring. In fact, there is generally a week in April or early May,--

"On such a time as goes before the leaf, When all the woods stand in a mist of green And nothing perfect,"--

during which the piping, voluble, rapid, intricate, and delicious warble of the ruby-crowned kinglet is the most noticeable strain to be heard, especially among the evergreens.

I notice that during the mating season of the birds the rivalries and jealousies are not all confined to the males. Indeed, the most spiteful and furious battles, as among the domestic fowls, are frequently between females. I have seen two hen robins scratch and pull feathers in a manner that contrasted strongly with the courtly and dignified sparring usual between the males. One March a pair of bluebirds decided to set up housekeeping in the trunk of an old apple-tree near my house. Not long after, an unwedded female appeared, and probably tried to supplant the lawful wife. I did not see what arts she used, but I saw her being very roughly handled by the jealous bride. The battle continued nearly all day about the orchard and grounds, and was a battle at very close quarters. The two birds would clinch in the air or on a tree, and fall to the ground with beaks and claws locked. The male followed them about, and warbled and called, but whether deprecatingly or encouragingly, I could not tell. Occasionally he would take a hand, but whether to separate them or whether to fan the flames, that I could not tell. So far as I could see, he was highly amused, and culpably indifferent to the issue of the battle.

The English spring begins much earlier than ours in New England and New York, yet an exceptionally early April with us must be nearly, if not quite, abreast with April as it usually appears in England. The blackthorn sometimes blooms in Britain in February, but the swallow does not appear till about the 20th of April, nor the anemone bloom ordinarily till that date. The nightingale comes about the same time, and the cuckoo follows close. Our cuckoo does not come till near June; but the water-thrush, which Audubon thought nearly equal to the nightingale as a songster (though it certainly is not), I have known to come by the 21st. I have seen the sweet English violet, escaped from the garden, and growing wild by the roadside, in bloom on the 25th of March, which is about, its date of flowering at home. During the same season, the first of our native flowers to appear was the hepatica, which I found on April 4. The arbutus and the dicentra appeared on the 10th, and the coltsfoot--which, however, is an importation--about the same time. The bloodroot, claytonia, saxifrage, and anemone were in bloom on the 17th, and I found the first blue violet and the great spurred violet on the 19th (saw the little violet-colored butterfly, dancing about the woods the same day). I plucked my first dandelion on a meadow slope on the 23d, and in the woods, protected by a high ledge, my first trillium. During the month at least twenty native shrubs and wild flowers bloomed in my vicinity, which is an unusual showing for April.

There are many things left for May, but nothing fairer, if as fair, as the first flower, the hepatica. I find I have never admired this little firstling half enough. When at the maturity of its charms, it is certainly the gem of the woods. What an individuality it has! No two clusters alike; all shades and sizes; some are snow-white, some pale pink, with just a tinge of violet, some deep purple, others the purest blue, others blue touched with lilac. A solitary blue-purple one, fully expanded and rising over the brown leaves or the green moss, its cluster of minute anthers showing like a group of pale stars on its little firmament, is enough to arrest and hold the dullest eye. Then, as I have elsewhere stated, there are individual hepaticas, or individual families among them, that are sweet-scented. The gift seems as capricious as the gift of genius in families. You cannot tell which the fragrant ones are till you try them. Sometimes it is the large white ones, sometimes the large purple ones, sometimes the small pink ones. The odor is faint, and recalls that of the sweet violets. A correspondent, who seems to have carefully observed these fragrant hepaticas, writes me that this gift of odor is constant in the same plant; that the plant which bears sweet-scented flowers this year will bear them next.

There is a brief period in our spring when I like more than at any other time to drive along the country roads, or even to be shot along by steam and have the landscape presented to me like a map. It is at that period, usually late in April, when we behold the first quickening of the earth. The waters have subsided, the roads have become dry, the sunshine has grown strong and its warmth has penetrated the sod; there is a stir of preparation about the farm and all through the country. One does not care to see things very closely: his interest in nature is not special but general. The earth is coming to life again. All the genial and more fertile places in the landscape are brought out; the earth is quickened in spots and streaks; you can see at a glance where man and nature have dealt the most kindly with it. The warm, moist places, the places that have had the wash of some building or of the road, or have been subjected to some special mellowing influence, how quickly the turf awakens there and shows the tender green! See what the landscape would be, how much earlier spring would come to it, if every square yard of it was alike moist and fertile. As the later snows lay in patches here and there, so now the earliest verdure is irregularly spread over the landscape, and is especially marked on certain slopes, as if it had blown over from the other side and lodged there.

A little earlier the homesteads looked cold and naked; the old farmhouse was bleak and unattractive; now Nature seems especially to smile upon it; her genial influences crowd up around it; the turf awakens all about as if in the spirit of friendliness. See the old barn on the meadow slope; the green seems to have oozed out from it, and to have flowed slowly down the hill; at a little distance it is lost in the sere stubble. One can see where every spring lies buried about the fields; its influence is felt at the surface, and the turf is early quickened there. Where the cattle have loved to lie and ruminate in the warm summer twilight, there the April sunshine loves to linger too, till the sod thrills to new life.

The home, the domestic feeling in nature, is brought out and enhanced at this time; what man has done tells, especially what he has done well. Our interest centres in the farmhouses, and in the influence that seems to radiate from there. The older the home, the more genial nature looks about it. The new architectural palace of the rich citizen, with the barns and outbuildings concealed or disguised as much as possible,--spring is in no hurry about it; the sweat of long years of honest labor has not yet fattened the soil it stands upon.

The full charm of this April landscape is not brought out till the afternoon. It seems to need the slanting rays of the evening sun to give it the right mellowness and tenderness, or the right perspective. It is, perhaps, a little too bald in the strong white light of the earlier part of the day; but when the faint four-o'clock shadows begin to come out, and we look through the green vistas and along the farm lanes toward the west, or out across long stretches of fields above which spring seems fairly hovering, just ready to alight, and note the teams slowly plowing, the brightened mould-board gleaming in the sun now and then,--it is at such times we feel its fresh, delicate attraction the most. There is no foliage on the trees yet; only here and there the red bloom of the soft maple, illuminated by the declining sun shows vividly against the tender green of a slope beyond, or a willow, like a thin veil, stands out against a leafless wood. Here and there a little meadow watercourse is golden with marsh marigolds, or some fence border, or rocky streak of neglected pasture land is thickly starred with the white flowers of the bloodroot. The eye can devour a succession of landscapes at such a time; there is nothing that sates or entirely fills it, but every spring token stimulates it, and makes it more on the alert.

April, too, is the time to go budding. A swelling bud is food for the fancy, and often food for the eye. Some buds begin to glow as they begin to swell. The bud scales change color and become a delicate rose pink. I note this especially in the European maple. The bud scales flush as if the effort to "keep in" brought the blood into their faces. The scales of the willow do not flush, but shine like ebony, and each one presses like a hand upon the catkin that will escape from beneath it.

When spring pushes pretty hard, many buds begin to sweat as well as to glow; they exude a brown, fragrant, gummy substance that affords the honey-bee her first cement and hive varnish. The hickory, the horse-chestnut, the plane-tree, the poplars, are all coated with this April myrrh. That of certain poplars, like the Balm of Gilead, is the most noticeable and fragrant,--no spring incense more agreeable. Its perfume is often upon the April breeze. I pick up the bud scales of the poplars along the road, long brown scales like the beaks of birds, and they leave a rich gummy odor in my hand that lasts for hours. I frequently detect the same odor about my hives when the bees are making all snug against the rains, or against the millers. When used by the bees, we call it propolis. Virgil refers to it as a "glue more adhesive than bird-lime and the pitch of Phrygian Ida." Pliny says it is extracted from the tears of the elm, the willow, and the reed. The bees often have serious work to detach it from their leg-baskets, and make it stick only where they want it to.

The bud scales begin to drop in April, and by May Day the scales have fallen from the eyes of every branch in the forest. In most cases the bud has an inner wrapping that does not fall so soon. In the hickory this inner wrapping is like a great livid membrane, an inch or more in length, thick, fleshy, and shining. It clasps the tender leaves about as if both protecting and nursing them. As the leaves develop, these membranous wrappings curl back, and finally wither and fall. In the plane-tree, or sycamore, this inner wrapping of the bud is a little pelisse of soft yellow or tawny fur. When it is cast off, it is the size of one's thumb nail, and suggests the delicate skin of some golden-haired mole. The young sycamore balls lay aside their fur wrappings early in May. The flower tassels of the European maple, too, come packed in a slightly furry covering. The long and fleshy inner scales that enfold the flowers and leaves are of a clear olive green, thinly covered with silken hairs like the young of some animals. Our sugar maple is less striking and beautiful in the bud, but the flowers are more graceful and fringelike.

Some trees have no bud scales. The sumac presents in early spring a mere fuzzy knot, from which, by and by, there emerges a soft, furry, tawny-colored kitten's paw. I know of nothing in vegetable nature that seems so really to be born as the ferns. They emerge from the ground rolled up, with a rudimentary and "touch-me-not" look, and appear to need a maternal tongue to lick them into shape. The sun plays the wet-nurse to them, and very soon they are out of that uncanny covering in which they come swathed, and take their places with other green things.

The bud scales strew the ground in spring as the leaves do in the fall, though they are so small that we hardly notice them. All growth, all development, is a casting off, a leaving of something behind. First the bud scales drop, then the flower drops, then the fruit drops, then the leaf drops.

The first two are preparatory and stand for spring; the last two are the crown and stand for autumn. Nearly the same thing happens with the seed in the ground. First the shell, or outer husk, is dropped or cast off; then the cotyledons, those nurse leaves of the young plant; then the fruit falls, and at last the stalk and leaf. A bud is a kind of seed planted in the branch instead of in the soil. It bursts and grows like a germ. In the absence of seeds and fruit, many birds and animals feed upon buds. The pine grosbeaks from the north are the most destructive budders that come among us. The snow beneath the maples they frequent is often covered with bud scales. The ruffed grouse sometimes buds in an orchard near the woods, and thus takes the farmer's apple crop a year in advance. Grafting is but a planting of buds. The seed is a complete, independent bud; it has the nutriment of the young plant within itself, as the egg holds several good lunches for the young chick. When the spider, or the wasp, or the carpenter bee, or the sand hornet lays an egg in a cell, and deposits food near it for the young when hatched, it does just what nature does in every kernel of corn or wheat, or bean, or nut. Around or within the chit or germ, she stores food for the young plant. Upon this it feeds till the root takes hold of the soil and draws sustenance from thence. The bud is rooted in the branch, and draws its sustenance from the milk of the pulpy cambium layer beneath the bark.

Another pleasant feature of spring, which I have not mentioned, is the full streams. Riding across the country one bright day in March, I saw and felt, as if for the first time, what an addition to the satisfaction one has in the open air at this season are the clear, full watercourses. They come to the front, as it were, and lure and hold the eye. There are no weeds, or grasses, or foliage to hide them; they are full to the brim, and fuller; they catch and reflect the sunbeams, and are about the only objects of life and motion in nature. The trees stand so still, the fields are so hushed and naked, the mountains so exposed and rigid, that the eye falls upon the blue, sparkling, undulating watercourses with a peculiar satisfaction. By and by the grass and trees will be waving, and the streams will be shrunken and hidden, and our delight will not be in them. The still ponds and lakelets will then please us more.

The little brown brooks,--how swift and full they ran! One fancied something gleeful and hilarious in them. And the large creeks,--how steadily they rolled on, trailing their ample skirts along the edges of the fields and marshes, and leaving ragged patches of water here and there! Many a gentle slope spread, as it were, a turfy apron in which reposed a little pool or lakelet. Many a stream sent little detachments across lots, the sparkling water seeming to trip lightly over the unbroken turf. Here and there an oak or an elm stood knee-deep in a clear pool, as if rising from its bath. It gives one a fresh, genial feeling to see such a bountiful supply of pure, running water. One's desires and affinities go out toward the full streams. How many a parched place they reach and lap in one's memory! How many a vision of naked pebbles and sun-baked banks they cover and blot out! They give eyes to the fields; they give dimples and laughter; they give light and motion. Running water! What a delightful suggestion the words always convey! One's thoughts and sympathies are set flowing by them; they unlock a fountain of pleasant fancies and associations in one's memory; the imagination is touched and refreshed.

March water is usually clean, sweet water; every brook is a trout-brook, a mountain brook; the cold and the snow have supplied the condition of a high latitude; no stagnation, no corruption, comes downstream now as on a summer freshet. Winter comes down, liquid and repentant. Indeed, it is more than water that runs then: it is frost subdued; it is spring triumphant. No obsolete watercourses now. The larger creeks seek out their abandoned beds, return to the haunts of their youth, and linger fondly there. The muskrat is adrift, but not homeless; his range is vastly extended, and he evidently rejoices in full streams. Through the tunnel of the meadow-mouse the water rushes as through a pipe; and that nest of his, that was so warm and cosy beneath the snowbank in the meadow-bottom, is sodden or afloat. But meadow-mice are not afraid of water. On various occasions I have seen them swimming about the spring pools like muskrats, and, when alarmed, diving beneath the water. Add the golden willows to the full streams, with the red-shouldered starlings perched amid their branches, sending forth their strong, liquid, gurgling notes, and the picture is complete. The willow branches appear to have taken on a deeper yellow in spring; perhaps it is the effect of the stronger sunshine, perhaps it is the effect of the swift, vital water laving their roots. The epaulettes of the starlings, too, are brighter than when they left us in the fall, and they appear to get brighter daily until the nesting begins. The males arrive many days before the females, and, perched along the marshes and watercourses, send forth their liquid, musical notes, passing the call from one to the other, as if to guide and hurry their mates forward.

The noise of a brook, you may observe, is by no means in proportion to its volume. The full March streams make far less noise relatively to their size than the shallower streams of summer, because the rocks and pebbles that cause the sound in summer are deeply buried beneath the current. "Still waters run deep" is not so true as "deep waters run still." I rode for half a day along the upper Delaware, and my thoughts almost unconsciously faced toward the full, clear river. Both the Delaware and the Susquehanna have a starved, impoverished look in summer,-- unsightly stretches of naked drift and bare, bleaching rocks. But behold them in March, after the frost has turned over to them the moisture it has held back and stored up as the primitive forests used to hold the summer rains. Then they have an easy, ample, triumphant look, that is a feast to the eye. A plump, well-fed stream is as satisfying to behold as a well-fed animal or a thrifty tree. One source of charm in the English landscape is the full, placid stream the season through; no desiccated watercourses will you see there, nor any feeble, decrepit brooks, hardly able to get over the ground.

This condition of our streams and rivers in spring is evidently but a faint reminiscence of their condition during what we may call the geological springtime, the March or April of the earth's history, when the annual rainfall appears to have been vastly greater than at present, and when the watercourses were consequently vastly larger and fuller. In pleistocene days the earth's climate was evidently much damper than at present. It was the rainiest of March weather. On no other theory can we account for the enormous erosion of the earth's surface, and the plowing of the great valleys. Professor Newberry finds abundant evidence that the Hudson was, in former times, a much larger river than now. Professor Zittel reaches the same conclusion concerning the Nile, and Humboldt was impressed with the same fact while examining the Orinoco and the tributaries of the Amazon. All these rivers appear to be but mere fractions of their former selves. The same is true of all the great lakes. If not Noah's flood, then evidently some other very wet spell, of which this is a tradition, lies far behind us. Something like the drought of summer is beginning upon the earth; the great floods have dried up; the rivers are slowly shrinking; the water is penetrating farther and farther into the cooling crust of the earth; and what was ample to drench and cover its surface, even to make a Noah's flood, will be but a drop in the bucket to the vast interior of the cooled sphere.

IV

APRIL

If we represent the winter of our northern climate by a rugged snow-clad mountain, and summer by a broad fertile plain, then the intermediate belt, the hilly and breezy uplands, will stand for spring, with March reaching well up into the region of the snows, and April lapping well down upon the greening fields and unloosened currents, not beyond the limits of winter's sallying storms, but well within the vernal zone,--within the reach of the warm breath and subtle, quickening influences of the plain below. At its best, April is the tenderest of tender salads made crisp by ice or snow water. Its type is the first spear of grass. The senses--sight, hearing, smell-- are as hungry for its delicate and almost spiritual tokens as the cattle are for the first bite of its fields. How it touches one and makes him both glad and sad! The voices of the arriving birds, the migrating fowls, the clouds of pigeons sweeping across the sky or filling the woods, the elfin horn of the first honey-bee venturing abroad in the middle of the day, the clear piping of the little frogs in the marshes at sundown, the camp-fire in the sugar-bush, the smoke seen afar rising over the trees, the tinge of green that comes so suddenly on the sunny knolls and slopes, the full translucent streams, the waxing and warming sun,--how these things and others like them are noted by the eager eye and ear! April is my natal month, and I am born again into new delight and new surprises at each return of it. Its name has an indescribable charm to me. Its two syllables are like the calls of the first birds,--like that of the phoebe-bird, or of the meadow-lark. Its very snows are fertilizing, and are called the poor man's manure.

Then its odors! I am thrilled by its fresh and indescribable odors,--the perfume of the bursting sod, of the quickened roots and rootlets, of the mould under the leaves, of the fresh furrows. No other month has odors like it. The west wind the other day came fraught with a perfume that was to the sense of smell what a wild and delicate strain of music is to the ear. It was almost transcendental. I walked across the hill with my nose in the air taking it in. It lasted for two days. I imagined it came from the willows of a distant swamp, whose catkins were affording the bees their first pollen; or did it come from much farther,--from beyond the horizon, the accumulated breath of innumerable farms and budding forests? The main characteristic of these April odors is their uncloying freshness. They are not sweet, they are oftener bitter, they are penetrating and lyrical. I know well the odors of May and June, of the world of meadows and orchards bursting into bloom, but they are not so ineffable and immaterial and so stimulating to the sense as the incense of April.

The season of which I speak does not correspond with the April of the almanac in all sections of our vast geography. It answers to March in Virginia and Maryland, while in parts of New York and New England it laps well over into May. It begins when the partridge drums, when the hyla pipes, when the shad start up the rivers, when the grass greens in the spring runs, and it ends when the leaves are unfolding and the last snowflake dissolves in mid-air. It may be the first of May before the first swallow appears, before the whippoorwill is heard, before the wood thrush sings; but it is April as long as there is snow upon the mountains, no matter what the almanac may say. Our April is, in fact, a kind of Alpine summer, full of such contrasts and touches of wild, delicate beauty as no other season affords. The deluded citizen fancies there is nothing enjoyable in the country till June, and so misses the freshest, tenderest part. It is as if one should miss strawberries and begin his fruit-eating with melons and peaches. These last are good,-- supremely so, they are melting and luscious,--but nothing so thrills and penetrates the taste, and wakes up and teases the papilla of the tongue, as the uncloying strawberry. What midsummer sweetness half so distracting as its brisk sub-acid flavor, and what splendor of full-leaved June can stir the blood like the best of leafless April?

One characteristic April feature, and one that delights me very much, is the perfect emerald of the spring runs while the fields are yet brown and sere,--strips and patches of the most vivid velvet green on the slopes and in the valleys. How the eye grazes there, and is filled and refreshed! I had forgotten what a marked feature this was until I recently rode in an open wagon for three days through a mountainous, pastoral country, remarkable for its fine springs. Those delicious green patches are yet in my eye. The fountains flowed with May. Where no springs occurred, there were hints and suggestions of springs about the fields and by the roadside in the freshened grass,--sometimes overflowing a space in the form of an actual fountain. The water did not quite get to the surface in such places, but sent its influence.

The fields of wheat and rye, too, how they stand out of the April landscape,--great green squares on a field of brown or gray!

Among April sounds there is none more welcome or suggestive to me than the voice of the little frogs piping in the marshes. No bird-note can surpass it as a spring token; and as it is not mentioned, to my knowledge, by the poets and writers of other lands, I am ready to believe it is characteristic of our season alone. You may be sure April has really come when this little amphibian creeps out of the mud and inflates its throat. We talk of the bird inflating its throat, but you should see this tiny minstrel inflate its throat, which becomes like a large bubble, and suggests a drummer-boy with his drum slung very high. In this drum, or by the aid of it, the sound is produced. Generally the note is very feeble at first, as if the frost was not yet all out of the creature's throat, and only one voice will be heard, some prophet bolder than all the rest, or upon whom the quickening ray of spring has first fallen. And it often happens that he is stoned for his pains by the yet unpacified element, and is compelled literally to "shut up" beneath a fall of snow or a heavy frost. Soon, however, he lifts up his voice again with more confidence, and is joined by others and still others, till in due time, say toward the last of the month, there is a shrill musical uproar, as the sun is setting, in every marsh and bog in the land. It is a plaintive sound, and I have heard people from the city speak of it as lonesome and depressing, but to the lover of the country it is a pure spring melody. The little piper will sometimes climb a bulrush, to which he clings like a sailor to a mast, and send forth his shrill call. There is a Southern species, heard when you have reached the Potomac, whose note is far more harsh and crackling. To stand on the verge of a swamp vocal with these, pains and stuns the ear. The call of the Northern species is far more tender and musical.[1]

[1] The Southern species is called the green hyla. I have since heard them in my neighborhood on the Hudson.

Then is there anything like a perfect April morning? One hardly knows what the sentiment of it is, but it is something very delicious. It is youth and hope. It is a new earth and a new sky. How the air transmits sounds, and what an awakening, prophetic character all sounds have! The distant barking of a dog, or the lowing of a cow, or the crowing of a cock, seems from out the heart of Nature, and to be a call to come forth. The great sun appears to have been reburnished, and there is something in his first glance above the eastern hills, and the way his eye-beams dart right and left and smite the rugged mountains into gold, that quickens the pulse and inspires the heart.

Across the fields in the early morning I hear some of the rare April birds,--the chewink and the brown thrasher. The robin, bluebird, song sparrow, phoebe-bird, etc., come in March; but these two ground-birds are seldom heard till toward the last of April. The ground-birds are all tree-singers or air singers; they must have an elevated stage to speak from. Our long-tailed thrush, or thrasher, like its congeners the catbird and mocking-bird, delights in a high branch of some solitary tree, whence it will pour out its rich and intricate warble for an hour together. This bird is the great American chipper. There is no other bird that I know of that can chip with such emphasis and military decision as this yellow-eyed songster. It is like the click of a giant gun-lock. Why is the thrasher so stealthy? It always seems to be going about on tiptoe. I never knew it to steal anything, and yet it skulks and hides like a fugitive from justice. One never sees it flying aloft in the air and traversing the world openly, like most birds, but it darts along fences and through bushes as if pursued by a guilty conscience. Only when the musical fit is upon it does it come up into full view, and invite the world to hear and behold.

The chewink is a shy bird also, but not stealthy. It is very inquisitive, and sets up a great scratching among the leaves, apparently to attract your attention. The male is perhaps the most conspicuously marked of all the ground-birds except the bobolink, being black above, bay on the sides, and white beneath. The bay is in compliment to the leaves he is forever scratching among,--they have rustled against his breast and sides so long that these parts have taken their color; but whence come the white and black? The bird seems to be aware that his color betrays him, for there are few birds in the woods so careful about keeping themselves screened from view. When in song, its favorite perch is the top of some high bush near to cover. On being disturbed at such times, it pitches down into the brush and is instantly lost to view.

This is the bird that Thomas Jefferson wrote to Wilson about, greatly exciting the latter's curiosity. Wilson was just then upon the threshold of his career as an ornithologist, and had made a drawing of the Canada jay, which he sent to the President. It was a new bird, and in reply Jefferson called his attention to a "curious bird" which was everywhere to be heard, but scarcely ever to be seen. He had for twenty years interested the young sportsmen of his neighborhood to shoot one for him, but without success. "It is in all the forests, from spring to fall," he says in his letter, "and never but on the tops of the tallest trees, from which it perpetually serenades us with some of the sweetest notes, and as clear as those of the nightingale. I have followed it for miles, without ever but once getting a good view of it. It is of the size and make of the mocking-bird, lightly thrush-colored on the back, and a grayish white on the breast and belly. Mr. Randolph, my son-in-law, was in possession of one which had been shot by a neighbor," etc. Randolph pronounced it a flycatcher, which was a good way wide of the mark. Jefferson must have seen only the female, after all his tramp, from his description of the color; but he was doubtless following his own great thoughts more than the bird, else he would have had an earlier view. The bird was not a new one, but was well known then as the ground-robin. The President put Wilson on the wrong scent by his erroneous description, and it was a long time before the latter got at the truth of the case. But Jefferson's letter is a good sample of those which specialists often receive from intelligent persons who have seen or heard something in their line very curious or entirely new, and who set the man of science agog by a description of the supposed novelty,--a description that generally fits the facts of the case about as well as your coat fits the chairback. Strange and curious things in the air, and in the water, and in the earth beneath, are seen every day except by those who are looking for them, namely, the naturalists. When Wilson or Audubon gets his eye on the unknown bird, the illusion vanishes, and your phenomenon turns out to be one of the commonplaces of the fields or woods.

A prominent April bird, that one does not have to go to the woods or away from his own door to see and hear, is the hardy and ever-welcome meadow-lark. What a twang there is about this bird, and what vigor! It smacks of the soil. It is the winged embodiment of the spirit of our spring meadows. What emphasis in its "z-d-t, z-d-t," and what character in its long, piercing note! Its straight, tapering, sharp beak is typical of its voice. Its note goes like a shaft from a crossbow; it is a little too sharp and piercing when near at hand, but, heard in the proper perspective, it is eminently melodious and pleasing. It is one of the major notes of the fields at this season. In fact, it easily dominates all others. "Spring o' the year! spring o' the year!" it says, with a long-drawn breath, a little plaintive, but not complaining or melancholy. At times it indulges in something much more intricate and lark-like while hovering on the wing in mid-air, but a song is beyond the compass of its instrument, and the attempt usually ends in a breakdown. A clear, sweet, strong, high-keyed note, uttered from some knoll or rock, or stake in the fence, is its proper vocal performance. It has the build and walk and flight of the quail and the grouse. It gets up before you in much the same manner, and falls an easy prey to the crack shot. Its yellow breast, surmounted by a black crescent, it need not be ashamed to turn to the morning sun, while its coat of mottled gray is in perfect keeping with the stubble amid which it walks.

The two lateral white quills in its tails seem strictly in character. These quills spring from a dash of scorn and defiance in the bird's make-up. By the aid of these, it can almost emit a flash as it struts about the fields and jerks out its sharp notes. They give a rayed, a definite and piquant expression to its movements. This bird is not properly a lark, but a starling, say the ornithologists, though it is lark-like in its habits, being a walker and entirely a ground-bird. Its color also allies it to the true lark. I believe there is no bird in the English or European fields that answers to this hardy pedestrian of our meadows. He is a true American, and his note one of our characteristic

April sounds.

Another marked April note, proceeding sometimes from the meadows, but more frequently from the rough pastures and borders of the woods, is the call of the high-hole, or golden-shafted woodpecker. It is quite as strong as that of the meadow-lark, but not so long-drawn and piercing. It is a succession of short notes rapidly uttered, as if the bird said "if-if-if-if-if-if-if." The notes of the ordinary downy and hairy woodpeckers suggest, in some way, the sound of a steel punch; but that of the high-hole is much softer, and strikes on the ear with real springtime melody. The high-hole is not so much a wood-pecker as he is a ground-pecker. He subsists largely on ants and crickets, and does not appear till they are to be found.

In Solomon's description of spring, the voice of the turtle is prominent, but our turtle, or mourning dove, though it arrives in April, can hardly be said to contribute noticeably to the open-air sounds. Its call is so vague, and soft, and mournful,--in fact, so remote and diffused,--that few persons ever hear it at all.

Such songsters as the cow blackbird are noticeable at this season, though they take a back seat a little later. It utters a peculiarly liquid April sound. Indeed, one would think its crop was full of water, its notes so bubble up and regurgitate, and are delivered with such an apparent stomachic contraction. This bird is the only feathered polygamist we have. The females are greatly in excess of the males, and the latter are usually attended by three or four of the former. As soon as the other birds begin to build, they are on the qui vive, prowling about like gypsies, not to steal the young of others, but to steal their eggs into other birds' nests, and so shirk the labor and responsibility of hatching and rearing their own young. As these birds do not mate, and as therefore there can be little or no rivalry or competition between the males, one wonders--in view of Darwin's teaching--why one sex should have brighter and richer plumage than the other, which is the fact. The males are easily distinguished from the dull and faded females by their deep glossy-black coats.

The April of English literature corresponds nearly to our May. In Great Britain, the swallow and the cuckoo usually arrive by the middle of April; with us, their appearance is a week or two later. Our April, at its best, is a bright, laughing face under a hood of snow, like the English March, but presenting sharper contrasts, a greater mixture of smiles and tears and icy looks than are known to our ancestral climate. Indeed, Winter sometimes retraces his steps in this month, and unburdens himself of the snows that the previous cold has kept back; but we are always sure of a number of radiant, equable days,--days that go before the bud, when the sun embraces the earth with fervor and determination. How his beams pour into the woods till the mould under the leaves is warm and emits an odor! The waters glint and sparkle, the birds gather in groups, and even those unwont to sing find a voice. On the streets of the cities, what a flutter, what bright looks and gay colors! I recall one prominent day of this kind last April. I made a note of it in my notebook. The earth seemed suddenly to emerge from a wilderness of clouds and chilliness into one of these blue sunlit spaces. How the voyagers rejoiced! Invalids came forth, old men sauntered down the street, stocks went up, and the political outlook brightened.

Such days bring out the last of the hibernating animals. The woodchuck unrolls and creeps out of his den to see if his clover has started yet. The torpidity leaves the snakes and the turtles, and they come forth and bask in the sun. There is nothing so small, nothing so great, that it does not respond to these celestial spring days, and give the pendulum of life a fresh start.

April is also the month of the new furrow. As soon as the frost is gone and the ground settled, the plow is started upon the hill, and at each bout I see its brightened mould-board flash in the sun. Where the last remnants of the snowdrift lingered yesterday the plow breaks the sod to-day. Where the drift was deepest the grass is pressed flat, and there is a deposit of sand and earth blown from the fields to windward. Line upon line the turf is reversed, until there stands out of the neutral landscape a ruddy square visible for miles, or until the breasts of the broad hills glow like the breasts of the robins.

Then who would not have a garden in April? to rake together the rubbish and burn it up, to turn over the renewed soil, to scatter the rich compost, to plant the first seed or bury the first tuber! It is not the seed that is planted, any more than it is I that is planted; it is not the dry stalks and weeds that are burned up, any more than it is my gloom and regrets that are consumed. An April smoke makes a clean harvest.

I think April is the best month to be born in. One is just in time, so to speak, to catch the first train, which is made up in this month. My April chickens always turn out best. They get an early start; they have rugged constitutions. Late chickens cannot stand the heavy dews, or withstand the predaceous hawks. In April all nature starts with you. You have not come out your hibernaculum too early or too late; the time is ripe, and, if you do not keep pace with the rest, why, the fault is not in the season.

V

BIRCH BROWSINGS

The region of which I am about to speak lies in the southern part of the State of New York, and comprises parts of three counties,--Ulster, Sullivan, and Delaware. It is drained by tributaries of both the Hudson and Delaware, and, next to the Adirondack section, contains more wild land than any other tract in the State. The mountains which traverse it, and impart to it its severe northern climate, belong properly to the Catskill range. On some maps of the State they are called the Pine Mountains, though with obvious local impropriety, as pine, so far as I have observed, is nowhere found upon them. "Birch Mountains" would be a more characteristic name, as on their summits birch is the prevailing tree. They are the natural home of the black and yellow birch, which grow here to unusual size. On their sides beech and maple abound; while, mantling their lower slopes and darkening the valleys, hemlock formerly enticed the lumberman and tanner. Except in remote or inaccessible localities, the latter tree is now almost never found. In Shandaken and along the Esopus it is about the only product the country yielded, or is likely to yield. Tanneries by the score have arisen and flourished upon the bark, and some of them still remain. Passing through that region the present season, I saw that the few patches of hemlock that still lingered high up on the sides of the mountains were being felled and peeled, the fresh white boles of the trees, just stripped of their bark, being visible a long distance.

Among these mountains there are no sharp peaks, or abrupt declivities, as in a volcanic region, but long, uniform ranges, heavily timbered to their summits, and delighting the eye with vast, undulating horizon lines. Looking south from the heights about the head of the Delaware, one sees twenty miles away a continual succession of blue ranges, one behind the other. If a few large trees are missing on the sky line, one can see the break a long distance off.

Approaching this region from the Hudson River side, you cross a rough, rolling stretch of country, skirting the base of the Catskills, which from a point near Saugerties sweep inland; after a drive of a few hours you are within the shadow of a high, bold mountain, which forms a sort of butt-end to this part of the range, and which is simply called High Point. To the east and southeast it slopes down rapidly to the plain, and looks defiance toward the Hudson, twenty miles distant; in the rear of it, and radiating from it west and northwest, are numerous smaller ranges, backing up, as it were, this haughty chief.

From this point through to Pennsylvania, a distance of nearly one hundred miles, stretches the tract of which I speak. It is a belt of country from twenty to thirty miles wide, bleak and wild, and but sparsely settled. The traveler on the New York and Erie Railroad gets a glimpse of it.

Many cold, rapid trout streams, which flow to all points of the compass, have their source in the small lakes and copious mountain springs of this region. The names of some of them are Mill Brook, Dry Brook, Willewemack, Beaver Kill, Elk Bush Kill, Panther Kill, Neversink, Big Ingin, and Callikoon. Beaver Kill is the main outlet on the west. It joins the Delaware in the wilds of Hancock. The Neversink lays open the region to the south, and also joins the Delaware. To the east, various Kills unite with the Big Ingin to form the Esopus, which flows into the Hudson. Dry Brook and Mill Brook, both famous trout streams, from twelve to fifteen miles long, find their way into the Delaware.

The east or Pepacton branch of the Delaware itself takes its rise near here in a deep pass between the mountains. I have many times drunk at a copious spring by the roadside, where the infant river first sees the light. A few yards beyond, the water flows the other way, directing its course through the Bear Kill and Schoharie Kill into the Mohawk.

Such game and wild animals as still linger in the State are found in this region. Bears occasionally make havoc among the sheep. The clearings at the head of a valley are oftenest the scene of their depredations.

Wild pigeons, in immense numbers, used to breed regularly in the valley of the Big Ingin and about the head of the Neversink. The treetops for miles were full of their nests, while the going and coming of the old birds kept up a constant din. But the gunners soon got wind of it, and from far and near were wont to pour in during the spring, and to slaughter both old and young. This practice soon had the effect of driving the pigeons all away, and now only a few pairs breed in these woods.

Deer are still met with, though they are becoming scarcer every year. Last winter near seventy head were killed on the Beaver Kill alone. I heard of one wretch, who, finding the deer snowbound, walked up to them on his snowshoes, and one morning before breakfast slaughtered six, leaving their carcasses where they fell. There are traditions of persons having been smitten blind or senseless when about to commit some heinous offense, but the fact that this villain escaped without some such visitation throws discredit on all such stories.

The great attraction, however, of this region is the brook trout, with which the streams and lakes abound. The water is of excessive coldness, the thermometer indicating 44 and 45 in the springs, and 47 or 48 in the smaller streams. The trout are generally small, but in the more remote branches their number is very great. In such localities the fish are quite black, but in the lakes they are of a lustre and brilliancy impossible to describe.

These waters have been much visited of late years by fishing parties, and the name of Beaver Kill is now a potent word among New York sportsmen.

One lake, in the wilds of Callikoon, abounds in a peculiar species of white sucker, which is of excellent quality. It is taken only in spring, during the spawning season, at the time "when the leaves are as big as a chipmunk's ears." The fish run up the small streams and inlets, beginning at nightfall, and continuing till the channel is literally packed with them, and every inch of space is occupied. The fishermen pounce upon them at such times, and scoop them up by the bushel, usually wading right into the living mass and landing the fish with their hands. A small party will often secure in this manner a wagon load of fish. Certain conditions of the weather, as a warm south or southwest wind, are considered most favorable for the fish to run.

Though familiar all my life with the outskirts of this region, I have only twice dipped into its wilder portions. Once in 1860 a friend and myself traced the Beaver Kill to its source, and encamped by Balsam Lake. A cold and protracted rainstorm coming on, we were obliged to leave the woods before we were ready. Neither of us will soon forget that tramp by an unknown route over the mountains, encumbered as we were with a hundred and one superfluities which we had foolishly brought along to solace ourselves with in the woods; nor that halt on the summit, where we cooked and ate our fish in a drizzling rain; nor, again, that rude log house, with its sweet hospitality, which we reached just at nightfall on Mill Brook.

In 1868 a party of three of us set out for a brief trouting excursion to a body of water called Thomas's Lake, situated in the same chain of mountains. On this excursion, more particularly than on any other I have ever undertaken, I was taught how poor an Indian I should make, and what a ridiculous figure a party of men may cut in the woods when the way is uncertain and the mountains high.

We left our team at a farmhouse near the head of the Mill Brook, one June afternoon, and with knapsacks on our shoulders struck into the woods at the base of the mountain, hoping to cross the range that intervened between us and the lake by sunset. We engaged a good-natured but rather indolent young man, who happened to be stopping at the house, and who had carried a knapsack in the Union armies, to pilot us a couple of miles into the woods so as to guard against any mistakes at the outset. It seemed the easiest thing in the world to find the lake. The lay of the land was so simple, according to accounts, that I felt sure I could go to it in the dark. "Go up this little brook to its source on the side of the mountain," they said. "The valley that contains the lake heads directly on the other side." What could be easier! But on a little further inquiry, they said we should "bear well to the left" when we reached the top of the mountain. This opened the doors again: "bearing well to the left" was an uncertain performance in strange woods. We might bear so well to the left that it would bring us ill. But why bear to the left at all, if the lake was directly opposite? Well, not quite opposite; a little to the left. There were two or three other valleys that headed in near there. We could easily find the right one. But to make assurance doubly sure, we engaged a guide, as stated, to give us a good start, and go with us beyond the bearing-to-the-left point. He had been to the lake the winter before and knew the way. Our course, the first half hour, was along an obscure wood-road which had been used for drawing ash logs off the mountain in winter. There was some hemlock, but more maple and birch. The woods were dense and free from underbrush, the ascent gradual. Most of the way we kept the voice of the creek in our ear on the right. I approached it once, and found it swarming with trout. The water was as cold as one ever need wish. After a while the ascent grew steeper, the creek became a mere rill that issued from beneath loose, moss-covered rocks and stones, and with much labor and puffing we drew ourselves up the rugged declivity. Every mountain has its steepest point, which is usually near the summit, in keeping, I suppose, with the providence that makes the darkest hour just before day. It is steep, steeper, steepest, till you emerge on the smooth level or gently rounded space at the top, which the old ice-gods polished off so long ago.

We found this mountain had a hollow in its back where the ground was soft and swampy. Some gigantic ferns, which we passed through, came nearly to our shoulders. We passed also several patches of swamp honeysuckles, red with blossoms.

Our guide at length paused on a big rock where the land began to dip down the other way, and concluded that he had gone far enough, and that we would now have no difficulty in finding the lake. "It must lie right down there," he said, pointing with his hand. But it was plain that he was not quite sure in his own mind. He had several times wavered in his course, and had shown considerable embarrassment when bearing to the left across the summit. Still we thought little of it. We were full of confidence, and, bidding him adieu, plunged down the mountain-side, following a spring run that we had no doubt led to the lake.

In these woods, which had a southeastern exposure, I first began to notice the wood thrush. In coming up the other side I had not seen a feather of any kind, or heard a note. Now the golden trillide-de of the wood thrush sounded through the silent woods. While looking for a fish-pole about half way down the mountain, I saw a thrush's nest in a little sapling about ten feet from the ground.

After continuing our descent till our only guide, the spring run, became quite a trout brook, and its tiny murmur a loud brawl, we began to peer anxiously through the trees for a glimpse of the lake, or for some conformation of the land that would indicate its proximity. An object which we vaguely discerned in looking under the near trees and over the more distant ones proved, on further inspection, to be a patch of plowed ground. Presently we made out a burnt fallow near it. This was a wet blanket to our enthusiasm. No lake, no sport, no trout for supper that night. The rather indolent young man had either played us a trick, or, as seemed more likely, had missed the way. We were particularly anxious to be at the lake between sundown and dark, as at that time the trout jump most freely.

Pushing on, we soon emerged into a stumpy field, at the head of a steep valley, which swept around toward the west. About two hundred rods below us was a rude log house, with smoke issuing from the chimney. A boy came out and moved toward the spring with a pail in his hand. We shouted to him, when he turned and ran back into the house without pausing to reply. In a moment the whole family hastily rushed into the yard, and turned their faces toward us. If we had come down their chimney, they could not have seemed more astonished. Not making out what they said, I went down to the house, and learned to my chagrin that we were still on the Mill Brook side, having crossed only a spur of the mountain. We had not borne sufficiently to the left, so that the main range, which, at the point of crossing, suddenly breaks off to the southeast, still intervened between us and the lake. We were about five miles, as the water runs, from the point of starting, and over two from the lake. We must go directly back to the top of the range where the guide had left us, and then, by keeping well to the left, we would soon come to a line of marked trees, which would lead us to the lake. So, turning upon our trail, we doggedly began the work of undoing what we had just done,--in all cases a disagreeable task, in this case a very laborious one also. It was after sunset when we turned back, and before we had got half way up the mountain it began to be quite dark. We were often obliged to rest our packs against trees and take breath, which made our progress slow. Finally a halt was called, beside an immense flat rock which had paused in its slide down the mountain, and we prepared to encamp for the night. A fire was built, the rock cleared off, a small ration of bread served out, our accoutrements hung up out of the way of the hedgehogs that were supposed to infest the locality, and then we disposed ourselves for sleep. If the owls or porcupines (and I think I heard one of the latter in the middle of the night) reconnoitred our camp, they saw a buffalo robe spread upon a rock, with three old felt hats arranged on one side, and three pairs of sorry-looking cowhide boots protruding from the other.

When we lay down, there was apparently not a mosquito in the woods; but the "no-see-ems," as Thoreau's Indian aptly named the midges, soon found us out, and after the fire had gone down annoyed us very much. My hands and wrists suddenly began to smart and itch in a most unaccountable manner. My first thought was that they had been poisoned in some way. Then the smarting extended to my neck and face, even to my scalp, when I began to suspect what was the matter. So, wrapping myself up more thoroughly, and stowing my hands away as best I could, I tried to sleep, being some time behind my companions, who appeared not to mind the "no-see-ems." I was further annoyed by some little irregularity on my side of the couch. The chambermaid had not beaten it up well. One huge lump refused to be mollified, and each attempt to adapt it to some natural hollow in my own body brought only a moment's relief. But at last I got the better of this also, and slept. Late in the night I woke up, just in time to hear a golden-crowned thrush sing in a tree near by. It sang as loud and cheerily as at midday, and I thought myself after all quite in luck. Birds occasionally sing at night, just as the cock crows. I have heard the hairbird, and the note of the kingbird; and the ruffed grouse frequently drums at night.

At the first faint signs of day a wood-thrush sang, a few rods below us. Then after a little delay, as the gray light began to grow around, thrushes broke out in full song in all parts of the woods. I thought I had never before heard them sing so sweetly. Such a leisurely, golden chant!--it consoled us for all we had undergone. It was the first thing in order,--the worms were safe till after this morning chorus. I judged that the birds roosted but a few feet from the ground. In fact, a bird in all cases roosts where it builds, and the wood thrush occupies, as it were, the first story of the woods.

There is something singular about the distribution of the wood thrushes. At an earlier stage of my observations I should have been much surprised at finding it in these woods. Indeed, I had stated in print on two occasions that the wood thrush was not found in the higher lands of the Catskills, but that the hermit thrush and the veery, or Wilson's thrush, were common. It turns out that this statement is only half true. The wood thrush is found also, but is much more rare and secluded in its habits than either of the others, being seen only during the breeding season on remote mountains, and then only on their eastern and southern slopes. I have never yet in this region found the bird spending the season in the near and familiar woods, which is directly contrary to observations I have made in other parts of the State. So different are the habits of birds in different localities.

As soon as it was fairly light we were up and ready to resume our march. A small bit of bread-and-butter and a swallow or two of whiskey was all we had for breakfast that morning. Our supply of each was very limited, and we were anxious to save a little of both, to relieve the diet of trout to which we looked forward.

At an early hour we reached the rock where we had parted with the guide, and looked around us into the dense, trackless woods with many misgivings. To strike out now on our own hook, where the way was so blind and after the experience we had just had, was a step not to be carelessly taken. The tops of these mountains are so broad, and a short distance in the woods seems so far, that one is by no means master of the situation after reaching the summit. And then there are so many spurs and offshoots and changes of direction, added to the impossibility of making any generalization by the aid of the eye, that before one is aware of it he is very wide of his mark.

I remembered now that a young farmer of my acquaintance had told me how he had made a long day's march through the heart of this region, without path or guide of any kind, and had hit his mark squarely. He had been bark-peeling in Callikoon,--a famous country for bark,--and, having got enough of it, he desired to reach his home on Dry Brook without making the usual circuitous journey between the two places. To do this necessitated a march of ten or twelve miles across several ranges of mountains and through an unbroken forest,--a hazardous undertaking in which no one would join him. Even the old hunters who were familiar with the ground dissuaded him and predicted the failure of his enterprise. But having made up his mind, he possessed himself thoroughly of the topography of the country from the aforesaid hunters, shouldered his axe, and set out, holding a straight course through the woods, and turning aside for neither swamps, streams, nor mountains. When he paused to rest he would mark some object ahead of him with his eye, in order that on getting up again he might not deviate from his course. His directors had told him of a hunter's cabin about midway on his route, which if he struck he might be sure he was right. About noon this cabin was reached, and at sunset he emerged at the head of Dry Brook.

After looking in vain for the line of marked trees, we moved off to the left in a doubtful, hesitating manner, keeping on the highest ground and blazing the trees as we went. We were afraid to go down hill, lest we should descend too soon; our vantage-ground was high ground. A thick fog coming on, we were more bewildered than ever. Still we pressed forward, climbing up ledges and wading through ferns for about two hours, when we paused by a spring that issued from beneath an immense wall of rock that belted the highest part of the mountain. There was quite a broad plateau here, and the birch wood was very dense, and the trees of unusual size.

After resting and exchanging opinions, we all concluded that it was best not to continue our search encumbered as we were; but we were not willing to abandon it altogether, and I proposed to my companions to leave them beside the spring with our traps, while I made one thorough and final effort to find the lake. If I succeeded and desired them to come forward, I was to fire my gun three times; if I failed and wished to return, I would fire it twice, they of course responding.

So, filling my canteen from the spring, I set out again, taking the spring run for my guide. Before I had followed it two hundred yards it sank into the ground at my feet. I had half a mind to be superstitious and to believe that we were under a spell, since our guides played us such tricks. However, I determined to put the matter to a further test, and struck out boldly to the left. This seemed to be the keyword,--to the left, to the left. The fog had now lifted, so that I could form a better idea of the lay of the land. Twice I looked down the steep sides of the mountain, sorely tempted to risk a plunge. Still I hesitated and kept along on the brink. As I stood on a rock deliberating, I heard a crackling of the brush, like the tread of some large game, on a plateau below me. Suspecting the truth of the case, I moved stealthily down, and found a herd of young cattle leisurely browsing. We had several times crossed their trail, and had seen that morning a level, grassy place on the top of the mountain, where they had passed the night. Instead of being frightened, as I had expected, they seemed greatly delighted, and gathered around me as if to inquire the tidings from the outer world,--perhaps the quotations of the cattle market. They came up to me, and eagerly licked my hand, clothes, and gun. Salt was what they were after, and they were ready to swallow anything that contained the smallest percentage of it. They were mostly yearlings and as sleek as moles. They had a very gamy look. We were afterwards told that, in the spring, the farmers round about turn into these woods their young cattle, which do not come out again till fall. They are then in good condition,--not fat, like grass-fed cattle, but trim and supple, like deer. Once a month the owner hunts them up and salts them. They have their beats, and seldom wander beyond well-defined limits. It was interesting to see them feed. They browsed on the low limbs and bushes, and on the various plants, munching at everything without any apparent discrimination.

They attempted to follow me, but I escaped them by clambering down some steep rocks. I now found myself gradually edging down the side of the mountain, keeping around it in a spiral manner, and scanning the woods and the shape of the ground for some encouraging hint or sign. Finally the woods became more open, and the descent less rapid. The trees were remarkably straight and uniform in size. Black birches, the first I had seen, were very numerous. I felt encouraged. Listening attentively, I caught, from a breeze just lifting the drooping leaves, a sound that I willingly believed was made by a bullfrog. On this hint, I tore down through the woods at my highest speed. Then I paused and listened again. This time there was no mistaking it; it was the sound of frogs. Much elated, I rushed on. By and by I could hear them as I ran. Pthrung, Pthrung, croaked the old ones; pug, pug; shrilly joined in the smaller fry.

Then I caught, through the lower trees, a gleam of blue, which I first thought was distant sky. A second look and I knew it to be water, and in a moment more I stepped from the woods and stood upon the shore of the lake. I exulted silently. There it was at last, sparkling in the morning sun, and as beautiful as a dream. It was so good to come upon such open space and such bright hues, after wandering in the dim, dense woods! The eye is as delighted as an escaped bird, and darts gleefully from point to point.

The lake was a long oval, scarcely more than a mile in circumference, with evenly wooded shores, which rose gradually on all sides. After contemplating the scene for a moment, I stepped back into the woods, and, loading my gun as heavily as I dared, discharged it three times. The reports seemed to fill all the mountains with sound. The frogs quickly hushed, and I listened for the response. But no response came. Then I tried again and again, but without evoking an answer. One of my companions, however, who had climbed to the top of the high rocks in the rear of the spring, thought he heard faintly one report. It seemed an immense distance below him, and far around under the mountain. I knew I had come a long way, and hardly expected to be able to communicate with my companions in the manner agreed upon. I therefore started back, choosing my course without any reference to the circuitous route by which I had come, and loading heavily and firing at intervals. I must have aroused many long-dormant echoes from a Rip Van Winkle sleep. As my powder got low, I fired and halloed alternately, till I came near splitting both my throat and gun. Finally, after I had begun to have a very ugly feeling of alarm and disappointment, and to cast about vaguely for some course to pursue in the emergency that seemed near at hand,--namely, the loss of my companions now I had found the lake,--a favoring breeze brought me the last echo of a response. I rejoined with spirit, and hastened with all speed in the direction whence the sound had come, but, after repeated trials, failed to elicit another answering sound. This filled me with apprehension again. I feared that my friends had been misled by the reverberations, and I pictured them to myself hastening in the opposite direction. Paying little attention to my course, but paying dearly for my carelessness afterward, I rushed forward to undeceive them. But they had not been deceived, and in a few moments an answering shout revealed them near at hand. I heard their tramp, the bushes parted, and we three met again.

In answer to their eager inquiries, I assured them that I had seen the lake, that it was at the foot of the mountain, and that we could not miss it if we kept straight down from where we then were.

My clothes were soaked with perspiration, but I shouldered my knapsack with alacrity, and we began the descent. I noticed that the woods were much thicker, and had quite a different look from those I had passed through, but thought nothing of it, as I expected to strike the lake near its head, whereas I had before come out at its foot. We had not gone far when we crossed a line of marked trees, which my companions were disposed to follow. It intersected our course nearly at right angles, and kept along and up the side of the mountain. My impression was that it led up from the lake, and that by keeping our own course we should reach the lake sooner than if we followed this line.

About half way down the mountain, we could see through the interstices the opposite slope. I encouraged my comrades by telling them that the lake was between us and that, and not more than half a mile distant. We soon reached the bottom, where we found a small stream and quite an extensive alder swamp, evidently the ancient bed of a lake. I explained to my half-vexed and half-incredulous companions that we were probably above the lake, and that this stream must lead to it. "Follow it," they said; "we will wait here till we hear from you."

So I went on, more than ever disposed to believe that we were under a spell, and that the lake had slipped from my grasp after all. Seeing no favorable sign as I went forward, I laid down my accoutrements, and climbed a decayed beech that leaned out over the swamp and promised a good view from the top. As I stretched myself up to look around from the highest attainable branch, there was suddenly a loud crack at the root. With a celerity that would at least have done credit to a bear, I regained the ground, having caught but a momentary glimpse of the country, but enough to convince me no lake was near. Leaving all incumbrances here but my gun, I still pressed on, loath to be thus baffled. After floundering through another alder swamp for nearly half a mile, I flattered myself that I was close on to the lake. I caught sight of a low spur of the mountain sweeping around like a half-extended arm, and I fondly imagined that within its clasp was the object of my search. But I found only more alder swamp. After this region was cleared, the creek began to descend the mountain very rapidly. Its banks became high and narrow, and it went whirling away with a sound that seemed to my ears like a burst of ironical laughter. I turned back with a feeling of mingled disgust, shame, and vexation. In fact I was almost sick, and when I reached my companions, after an absence of nearly two hours, hungry, fatigued, and disheartened, I would have sold my interest in Thomas's Lake at a very low figure. For the first time, I heartily wished myself well out of the woods. Thomas might keep his lake, and the enchanters guard his possession! I doubted if he had ever found it the second time, or if any one else ever had.

My companions, who were quite fresh, and who had not felt the strain of baffled purpose as I had, assumed a more encouraging tone. After I had rested awhile, and partaken sparingly of the bread and whiskey, which in such an emergency is a great improvement on bread and water, I agreed to their proposition that we should make another attempt. As if to reassure us, a robin sounded his cheery call near by, and the winter wren, the first I had heard in these woods, set his music-box going, which fairly ran over with fine, gushing, lyrical sounds. There can be no doubt but this bird is one of our finest songsters. If it would only thrive and sing well when caged, like the canary, how far it would surpass that bird! It has all the vivacity and versatility of the canary, without any of its shrillness. Its song is indeed a little cascade of melody.

We again retraced our steps, rolling the stone, as it were, back up the mountain, determined to commit ourselves to the line of marked trees. These we finally reached, and, after exploring the country to the right, saw that bearing to the left was still the order. The trail led up over a gentle rise of ground, and in less than twenty minutes we were in the woods I had passed through when I found the lake. The error I had made was then plain; we had come off the mountain a few paces too far to the right, and so had passed down on the wrong side of the ridge, into what we afterwards learned was the valley of Alder Creek.

We now made good time, and before many minutes I again saw the mimic sky glance through the trees. As we approached the lake a solitary woodchuck, the first wild animal we had seen since entering the woods, sat crouched upon the root of a tree a few feet from the water, apparently completely nonplussed by the unexpected appearance of danger on the land side. All retreat was cut off, and he looked his fate in the face without flinching. I slaughtered him just as a savage would have done, and from the same motive,--I wanted his carcass to eat.

The mid-afternoon sun was now shining upon the lake, and a low, steady breeze drove the little waves rocking to the shore. A herd of cattle were browsing on the other side, and the bell of the leader sounded across the water. In these solitudes its clang was wild and musical.

To try the trout was the first thing in order. On a rude raft of logs which we found moored at the shore, and which with two aboard shipped about a foot of water, we floated out and wet our first fly in Thomas's Lake; but the trout refused to jump, and, to be frank, not more than a dozen and a half were caught during our stay. Only a week previous, a party of three had taken in a few hours all the fish they could carry out of the woods, and had nearly surfeited their neighbors with trout. But from some cause they now refused to rise, or to touch any kind of bait; so we fell to catching the sunfish, which were small but very abundant. Their nests were all along shore. A space about the size of a breakfast-plate was cleared of sediment and decayed vegetable matter, revealing the pebbly bottom, fresh and bright, with one or two fish suspended over the centre of it, keeping watch and ward. If an intruder approached, they would dart at him spitefully. These fish have the air of bantam cocks, and, with their sharp, prickly fins and spines and scaly sides, must be ugly customers in a hand-to-hand encounter with other finny warriors. To a hungry man they look about as unpromising as hemlock slivers, so thorny and thin are they; yet there is sweet meat in them, as we found that day.

Much refreshed, I set out with the sun low in the west to explore the outlet of the lake and try for trout there, while my companions made further trials in the lake itself. The outlet, as is usual in bodies of water of this kind, was very gentle and private. The stream, six or eight feet wide, flowed silently and evenly along for a distance of three or four rods, when it suddenly, as if conscious of its freedom, took a leap down some rocks. Thence, as far as I followed it, its descent was very rapid through a continuous succession of brief falls like so many steps down the mountain. Its appearance promised more trout than I found, though I returned to camp with a very respectable string.

Toward sunset I went round to explore the inlet, and found that as usual the stream wound leisurely through marshy ground. The water being much colder than in the outlet, the trout were more plentiful. As I was picking my way over the miry ground and through the rank growths, a ruffed grouse hopped up on a fallen branch a few paces before me, and, jerking his tail, threatened to take flight. But as I was at that moment gunless and remained stationary, he presently jumped down and walked away.

A seeker of birds, and ever on the alert for some new acquaintance, my attention was arrested, on first entering the swamp, by a bright, lively song, or warble, that issued from the branches overhead, and that was entirely new to me, though there was something in the tone of it that told me the bird was related to the wood-wagtail and to the water-wagtail or thrush. The strain was emphatic and quite loud, like the canary's, but very brief. The bird kept itself well secreted in the upper branches of the trees, and for a long time eluded my eye. I passed to and fro several times, and it seemed to break out afresh as I approached a certain little bend in the creek, and to cease after I had got beyond it; no doubt its nest was somewhere in the vicinity. After some delay the bird was sighted and brought down. It proved to be the small, or northern, water-thrush (called also the New York water-thrush),--a new bird to me. In size it was noticeably smaller than the large, or Louisiana, water-thrush, as described by Audubon, but in other respects its general appearance was the same. It was a great treat to me, and again I felt myself in luck.

This bird was unknown to the older ornithologists, and is but poorly described by the new. It builds a mossy nest on the ground, or under the edge of a decayed log. A correspondent writes me that he has found it breeding on the mountains in Pennsylvania. The large-billed water-thrush is much the superior songster, but the present species has a very bright and cheerful strain. The specimen I saw, contrary to the habits of the family, kept in the treetops like a warbler, and seemed to be engaged in catching insects.

The birds were unusually plentiful and noisy about the head of this lake; robins, blue jays, and woodpeckers greeted me with their familiar notes. The blue jays found an owl or some wild animal a short distance above me, and, as is their custom on such occasions, proclaimed it at the top of their voices, and kept on till the darkness began to gather in the woods.

I also heard here, as I had at two or three other points in the course of the day, the peculiar, resonant hammering of some species of woodpecker upon the hard, dry limbs. It was unlike any sound of the kind I had ever before heard, and, repeated at intervals through the silent woods, was a very marked and characteristic feature. Its peculiarity was the ordered succession of the raps, which gave it the character of a premeditated performance. There were first three strokes following each other rapidly, then two much louder ones with longer intervals between them. I heard the drumming here, and the next day at sunset at Furlow Lake, the source of Dry Brook, and in no instance was the order varied. There was melody in it, such as a woodpecker knows how to evoke from a smooth, dry branch. It suggested something quite as pleasing as the liveliest bird-song, and was if anything more woodsy and wild. As the yellow-bellied woodpecker was the most abundant species in these woods, I attributed it to him. It is the one sound that still links itself with those scenes in my mind.

At sunset the grouse began to drum in all parts of the woods about the lake. I could hear five at one time, thump, thump, thump, thump, thr-r-r-r-r-rr. It was a homely, welcome sound. As I returned to camp at twilight, along the shore of the lake, the frogs also were in full chorus. The older ones ripped out their responses to each other with terrific force and volume. I know of no other animal capable of giving forth so much sound, in proportion to its size, as a frog. Some of these seemed to bellow as loud as a two-year-old bull. They were of immense size, and very abundant. No frog-eater had ever been there. Near the shore we felled a tree which reached far out in the lake. Upon the trunk and branches the frogs had soon collected in large numbers, and gamboled and splashed about the half-submerged top, like a parcel of schoolboys, making nearly as much noise.

After dark, as I was frying the fish, a panful of the largest trout was accidentally capsized in the fire. With rueful countenances we contemplated the irreparable loss our commissariat had sustained by this mishap; but remembering there was virtue in ashes, we poked the half-consumed fish from the bed of coals and ate them, and they were good.

We lodged that night on a brush-heap and slept soundly. The green, yielding beech-twigs, covered with a buffalo robe, were equal to a hair mattress. The heat and smoke from a large fire kindled in the afternoon had banished every "no-see-em" from the locality, and in the morning the sun was above the mountain before we awoke.

I immediately started again for the inlet, and went far up the stream toward its source. A fair string of trout for breakfast was my reward. The cattle with the bell were at the head of the valley, where they had passed the night. Most of them were two-year-old steers. They came up to me and begged for salt, and scared the fish by their importunities.

We finished our bread that morning, and ate every fish we could catch, and about ten o'clock prepared to leave the lake. The weather had been admirable, and the lake was a gem, and I would gladly have spent a week in the neighborhood; but the question of supplies was a serious one, and would brook no delay.

When we reached, on our return, the point where we had crossed the line of marked trees the day before, the question arose whether we should still trust ourselves to this line, or follow our own trail back to the spring and the battlement of rocks on the top of the mountain, and thence to the rock where the guide had left us. We decided in favor of the former course. After a march of three quarters of an hour the blazed trees ceased, and we concluded we were near the point at which we had parted with the guide. So we built a fire, laid down our loads, and cast about on all sides for some clew as to our exact locality. Nearly an hour was consumed in this manner and without any result. I came upon a brood of young grouse, which diverted me for a moment. The old one blustered about at a furious rate, trying to draw all attention to herself, while the young ones, which were unable to fly, hid themselves. She whined like a dog in great distress, and dragged herself along apparently with the greatest difficulty. As I pursued her, she ran very nimbly, and presently flew a few yards. Then, as I went on, she flew farther and farther each time, till at last she got up, and went humming through the woods as if she had no interest in them. I went back and caught one of the young, which had simply squatted close to the leaves. I took it up and set it on the palm of my hand, which it hugged as closely as if still upon the ground. I then put it in my coat-sleeve, when it ran and nestled in my armpit.

When we met at the sign of the smoke, opinions differed as to the most feasible course. There was no doubt but that we could get out of the woods; but we wished to get out speedily, and as near as possible to the point where we had entered. Half ashamed of our timidity and indecision, we finally tramped away back to where we had crossed the line of blazed trees, followed our old trail to the spring on the top of the range, and, after much searching and scouring to the right and left, found ourselves at the very place we had left two hours before. Another deliberation and a divided council. But something must be done. It was then mid-afternoon, and the prospect of spending another night on the mountains, without food or drink, was not pleasant. So we moved down the ridge. Here another line of marked trees was found, the course of which formed an obtuse angle with the one we had followed. It kept on the top of the ridge for perhaps a mile, when it entirely disappeared, and we were as much adrift as ever. Then one of the party swore an oath, and said he was going out of those woods, hit or miss, and, wheeling to the right, instantly plunged over the brink of the mountain. The rest followed, but would fain have paused and ciphered away at their own uncertainties, to see if a certainty could not be arrived at as to where we would come out. But our bold leader was solving the problem in the right way. Down and down and still down we went, as if we were to bring up in the bowels of the earth. It was by far the steepest descent we had made, and we felt a grim satisfaction in knowing that we could not retrace our steps this time, be the issue what it might. As we paused on the brink of a ledge of rocks, we chanced to see through the trees distant cleared land. A house or barn was dimly descried. This was encouraging; but we could not make out whether it was on Beaver Kill or Mill Brook or Dry Brook, and did not long stop to consider where it was. We at last brought up at the bottom of a deep gorge, through which flowed a rapid creek that literally swarmed with trout. But we were in no mood to catch them, and pushed on along the channel of the stream, sometimes leaping from rock to rock, and sometimes splashing heedlessly through the water, and speculating the while as to where we should probably come out. On the Beaver Kill, my companions thought; but, from the position of the sun, I said, on the Mill Brook, about six miles below our team; for I remembered having seen, in coming up this stream, a deep, wild valley that led up into the mountains, like this one. Soon the banks of the stream became lower, and we moved into the woods. Here we entered upon an obscure wood-road, which presently conducted us into the midst of a vast hemlock forest. The land had a gentle slope, and we wondered why the lumbermen and barkmen who prowl through these woods had left this fine tract untouched. Beyond this the forest was mostly birch and maple.

We were now close to the settlement, and began to hear human sounds. One rod more, and we were out of the woods. It took us a moment to comprehend the scene. Things looked very strange at first; but quickly they began to change and to put on familiar features. Some magic scene-shifting seemed to take place before my eyes, till, instead of the unknown settlement which I at first seemed to look upon, there stood the farmhouse at which we had stopped two days before, and at the same moment we heard the stamping of our team in the barn. We sat down and laughed heartily over our good luck. Our desperate venture had resulted better than we had dared to hope, and had shamed our wisest plans. At the house our arrival had been anticipated about this time, and dinner was being put upon the table.

It was then five o'clock, so that we had been in the woods just forty-eight hours; but if time is only phenomenal, as the philosophers say, and life only in feeling, as the poets aver, we were some months, if not years, older at that moment than we had been two days before. Yet younger, too,--though this be a paradox,--for the birches had infused into us some of their own suppleness and strength.

VI

A BUNCH OF HERBS

FRAGRANT WILD FLOWERS

The charge that was long ago made against our wild flowers by English travelers in this country, namely, that they were odorless, doubtless had its origin in the fact that, whereas in England the sweet-scented flowers are among the most common and conspicuous, in this country they are rather shy and withdrawn, and consequently not such as travelers would be likely to encounter. Moreover, the British traveler, remembering the deliciously fragrant blue violets he left at home, covering every grassy slope and meadow bank in spring, and the wild clematis, or traveler's joy, overrunning hedges and old walls with its white, sweet-scented blossoms, and finding the corresponding species here equally abundant but entirely scentless, very naturally inferred that our wild flowers were all deficient in this respect. He would be confirmed in this opinion when, on turning to some of our most beautiful and striking native flowers, like the laurel, the rhododendron, the columbine, the inimitable fringed gentian, the burning cardinal-flower, or our asters and goldenrod, dashing the roadsides with tints of purple and gold, he found them scentless also. "Where are your fragrant flowers?" he might well say; "I can find none." Let him look closer and penetrate our forests, and visit our ponds and lakes. Let him compare our matchless, rosy-lipped, honey-hearted trailing arbutus with his own ugly ground-ivy; let him compare our sumptuous, fragrant pond-lily with his own odorless Nymphus alba. In our Northern woods he shall find the floors carpeted with the delicate linnus, its twin rose-colored nodding flowers filling the air with fragrance. (I am aware that the linnus is found in some parts of Northern Europe.) The fact is, we perhaps have as many sweet-scented wild flowers as Europe has, only they are not quite so prominent in our flora, nor so well known to our people or to our poets.

Think of Wordsworth's "Golden Daffodils:"--

"I wandered lonely as a cloud That floats on high o'er vales and hills, When all at once I saw a crowd, A host of golden daffodils, Beside the lake, beneath the trees, Fluttering and dancing in the breeze.

"Continuous as the stars that shine And twinkle on the milky way, They stretched in never-ending line Along the margin of a bay. Ten thousand saw I at a glance, Tossing their heads in sprightly dance."

No such sight could greet the poet's eye here. He might see ten thousand marsh marigolds, or ten times ten thousand houstonias, but they would not toss in the breeze, and they would not be sweet-scented like the daffodils.

It is to be remembered, too, that in the moister atmosphere of England the same amount of fragrance would be much more noticeable than with us. Think how our sweet bay, or our pink azalea, or our white alder, to which they have nothing that corresponds, would perfume that heavy, vapor-laden air!

In the woods and groves in England, the wild hyacinth grows very abundantly in spring, and in places the air is loaded with its fragrance. In our woods a species of dicentra, commonly called squirrel corn, has nearly the same perfume, and its racemes of nodding whitish flowers, tinged with red, are quite as pleasing to the eye, but it is a shyer, less abundant plant. When our children go to the fields in April and May, they can bring home no wild flowers as pleasing as the sweet English violet, and cowslip, and yellow daffodil, and wallflower; and when British children go to the woods at the same season, they can load their hands and baskets with nothing that compares with our trailing arbutus, or, later in the season, with our azaleas; and when their boys go fishing or boating in summer, they can wreathe themselves with nothing that approaches our pond-lily.

There are upward of forty species of fragrant native wild flowers and flowering shrubs and trees in New England and New York, and, no doubt, many more in the South and West. My list is as follows:--

White violet (Viola blanda). Canada violet (Viola Canadensis). Hepatica (occasionally fragrant). Trailing arbutus (Epig repens). Mandrake (Podophyllum peltatum). Yellow lady's-slipper (Cypripedium parviflorum). Purple lady's-slipper (Cypripedium acaule). Squirrel corn (Dicentra Canadensis). Showy orchis (Orchis spectabilis). Purple fringed-orchis (Habenaria psycodes). Arethusa (Arethusa bulbosa). Calopogon (Calopogon pulchellus). Lady's-tresses (Spiranthes cernua). Pond-lily (Nymphus odorata). Wild Rose (Rosa nitida). Twin-flower (Linn borealis). Sugar maple (Acer saccharinum). Linden (Tilia Americana). Locust-tree (Robinia pseudacacia). White-alder (Clethra alnifolia). Smooth azalea (Rhododendron arborescens). White azalea (Rhododendron viscosum). Pinxter-flower (Rhododendron nudiflorum). Yellow azalea (Rhododendron calendulaceum). Sweet bay (Magnolia glauca). Mitchella vine (Mitchella repens). Sweet coltsfoot (Petasites palmata). Pasture thistle (Cnicus pumilus). False wintergreen (Pyrola rotundifolia). Spotted wintergreen (Chimaphila maculata). Prince's pine (Chimaphila umbellata). Evening primrose (Oenothera biennis). Hairy loosestrife (Steironema ciliatum). Dogbane (Apocynum). Ground-nut (Apios tuberosa). Adder's-tongue pogonia (Pogonia ophioglossoides). Wild grape (Vitis cordifolia). Horned bladderwort (Utricularia cornuta).

The last-named, horned bladderwort, is perhaps the most fragrant flower we have. In a warm, moist atmosphere, its odor is almost too strong. It is a plant with a slender, leafless stalk or scape less than a foot high, with two or more large yellow hood or helmet shaped flowers. It is not common, and belongs pretty well north, growing in sandy swamps and along the marshy margins of lakes and ponds. Its perfume is sweet and spicy in an eminent degree. I have placed in the above list several flowers that are intermittently fragrant, like the hepatica, or liver-leaf. This flower is the earliest, as it is certainly one of the most beautiful, to be found in our woods, and occasionally it is fragrant. Group after group may be inspected--ranging through all shades of purple and blue, with some perfectly white--and no odor be detected, when presently you will happen upon a little brood of them that have a most delicate and delicious fragrance. The same is true of a species of loosestrife growing along streams and on other wet places, with tall bushy stalks, dark green leaves, and pale axillary yellow flowers (probably European). A handful of these flowers will sometimes exhale a sweet fragrance; at other times, or from another locality, they are scentless. Our evening primrose is thought to be uniformly sweet-scented, but the past season I examined many specimens, and failed to find one that was so. Some seasons the sugar maple yields much sweeter sap than in others; and even individual trees, owing to the soil, moisture, etc., where they stand, show a great difference in this respect. The same is doubtless true of the sweet-scented flowers. I had always supposed that our Canada violet--the tall, leafy-stemmed white violet of our Northern woods--was odorless, till a correspondent called my attention to the contrary fact. On examination I found that, while the first ones that bloomed about May 25 had very sweet-scented foliage, especially when crushed in the hand, the flowers were practically without fragrance. But as the season advanced the fragrance developed, till a single flower had a well-marked perfume, and a handful of them was sweet indeed. A single specimen, plucked about August 1, was quite as fragrant as the English violet, though the perfume is not what is known as violet, but, like that of the hepatica, comes nearer to the odor of certain fruit-trees.

It is only for a brief period that the blossoms of our sugar maple are sweet-scented; the perfume seems to become stale after a few days: but pass under this tree just at the right moment, say at nightfall on the first or second day of its perfect inflorescence, and the air is loaded with its sweetness; its perfumed breath falls upon you as its cool shadow does a few weeks later.

After the linn and the arbutus, the prettiest sweet-scented flowering vine our woods hold is the common mitchella vine, called squaw-berry and partridge-berry. It blooms in June, and its twin flowers, light cream-color, velvety, tubular, exhale a most agreeable fragrance.

Our flora is much more rich in orchids than the European, and many of ours are fragrant. The first to bloom in the spring is the showy orchis, though it is far less showy than several others. I find it in May, not on hills, where Gray says it grows, but in low, damp places in the woods. It has two oblong shining leaves, with a scape four or five inches high strung with sweet-scented, pink-purple flowers. I usually find it and the fringed polygala in bloom at the same time; the lady's-slipper is a little later. The purple fringed orchis, one of the most showy and striking of all our orchids, blooms in midsummer in swampy meadows and in marshy, grassy openings in the woods, shooting up a tapering column or cylinder of pink-purple fringed flowers, that one may see at quite a distance, and the perfume of which is too rank for a close room. This flower is, perhaps, like the English fragrant orchis, found in pastures.

Few fragrant flowers in the shape of weeds have come to us from the Old World, and this leads me to remark that plants with sweet-scented flowers are, for the most part, more intensely local, more fastidious and idiosyncratic, than those without perfume. Our native thistle--the pasture thistle--has a marked fragrance, and it is much more shy and limited in its range than the common Old World thistle that grows everywhere. Our little sweet white violet grows only in wet places, and the Canada violet only in high, cool woods, while the common blue violet is much more general in its distribution. How fastidious and exclusive is the cypripedium! You will find it in one locality in the woods, usually on high, dry ground, and will look in vain for it elsewhere. It does not go in herds like the commoner plants, but affects privacy and solitude. When I come upon it in my walks, I seem to be intruding upon some very private and exclusive company. The large yellow cypripedium has a peculiar, heavy, oily odor.

In like manner one learns where to look for arbutus, for pipsissewa, for the early orchis; they have their particular haunts, and their surroundings are nearly always the same. The yellow pond-lily is found in every sluggish stream and pond, but Nymphus odorata requires a nicer adjustment of conditions, and consequently is more restricted in its range. If the mullein were fragrant, or toad-flax, or the daisy, or blueweed, or goldenrod, they would doubtless be far less troublesome to the agriculturist. There are, of course, exceptions to the rule I have here indicated, but it holds in most cases. Genius is a specialty: it does not grow in every soil; it skips the many and touches the few; and the gift of perfume to a flower is a special grace like genius or like beauty, and never becomes common or cheap.

"Do honey and fragrance always go together in the flowers?" Not uniformly. Of the list of fragrant wild flowers I have given, the only ones that the bees procure nectar from, so far as I have observed, are arbutus, dicentra, sugar maple, locust, and linden. Non-fragrant flowers that yield honey are those of the raspberry, clematis, sumac, bugloss, ailanthus, goldenrod, aster, fleabane. A large number of odorless plants yield pollen to the bee. There is nectar in the columbine, and the bumblebee sometimes gets it by piercing the spur from the outside, as she does with the dicentra. There ought to be honey in the honeysuckle, but I have never seen the hive bee make any attempt to get it.

WEEDS

One is tempted to say that the most human plants, after all, are the weeds. How they cling to man and follow him around the world, and spring up wherever he sets his foot! How they crowd around his barns and dwellings, and throng his garden and jostle and override each other in their strife to be near him! Some of them are so domestic and familiar, and so harmless withal, that one comes to regard them with positive affection. Motherwort, catnip, plantain, tansy, wild mustard,--what a homely human look they have! they are an integral part of every old homestead. Your smart new place will wait long before they draw near it. Our knot-grass, that carpets every old dooryard, and fringes every walk, and softens every path that knows the feet of children, or that leads to the spring, or to the garden, or to the barn, how kindly one comes to look upon it! Examine it with a pocket glass and see how wonderfully beautiful and exquisite are its tiny blossoms. It loves the human foot, and when the path or the place is long disused other plants usurp the ground.

The gardener and the farmer are ostensibly the greatest enemies of the weeds, but they are in reality their best friends. Weeds, like rats and mice, increase and spread enormously in a cultivated country. They have better food, more sunshine, and more aids in getting themselves disseminated. They are sent from one end of the land to the other in seed grain of various kinds, and they take their share, and more too, if they can get it, of the phosphates and stable manures. How sure, also, they are to survive any war of extermination that is waged against them! In yonder field are ten thousand and one Canada thistles. The farmer goes resolutely to work and destroys ten thousand and thinks the work is finished, but he has done nothing till he has destroyed the ten thousand and one. This one will keep up the stock and again cover his fields with thistles.

Weeds are Nature's makeshift. She rejoices in the grass and the grain, but when these fail to cover her nakedness she resorts to weeds. It is in her plan or a part of her economy to keep the ground constantly covered with vegetation of some sort, and she has layer upon layer of seeds in the soil for this purpose, and the wonder is that each kind lies dormant until it is wanted. If I uncover the earth in any of my fields, ragweed and pigweed spring up; if these are destroyed, harvest grass, or quack grass, or purslane appears. The spade or plow that turns these under is sure to turn up some other variety, as chickweed, sheep-sorrel, or goose-foot. The soil is a storehouse of seeds.

The old farmers say that wood-ashes will bring in the white clover, and it will; the germs are in the soil wrapped in a profound slumber, but this stimulus tickles them until they awake. Stramonium has been known to start up on the site of an old farm building, when it had not been seen in that locality for thirty years. I have been told that a farmer, somewhere in New England, in digging a well came at a great depth upon sand like that of the seashore; it was thrown out, and in due time there sprang from it a marine plant. I have never seen earth taken from so great a depth that it would not before the end of the season be clothed with a crop of weeds. Weeds are so full of expedients, and the one engrossing purpose with them is to multiply. The wild onion multiplies at both ends,--at the top by seed, and at the bottom by offshoots. Toad-flax travels under ground and above ground. Never allow a seed to ripen, and yet it will cover your field. Cut off the head of the wild carrot, and in a week or two there are five heads in room of this one; cut off these, and by fall there are ten looking defiance at you from the same root. Plant corn in August, and it will go forward with its preparations as if it had the whole season before it. Not so with the weeds; they have learned better. If amaranth, or abutilon, or burdock gets a late start, it makes great haste to develop its seed; it foregoes its tall stalk and wide flaunting growth, and turns all its energies into keeping up the succession of the species. Certain fields under the plow are always infested with "blind nettles," others with wild buckwheat, black blindweed, or cockle. The seed lies dormant under the sward, the warmth and the moisture affect it not until other conditions are fulfilled.

The way in which one plant thus keeps another down is a great mystery. Germs lie there in the soil and resist the stimulating effect of the sun and the rains for years, and show no sign. Presently something whispers to them, "Arise, your chance has come; the coast is clear;" and they are up and doing in a twinkling.

Weeds are great travelers; they are, indeed, the tramps of the vegetable world. They are going east, west, north, south; they walk; they fly; they swim; they steal a ride; they travel by rail, by flood, by wind; they go under ground, and they go above, across lots, and by the highway. But, like other tramps, they find it safest by the highway: in the fields they are intercepted and cut off; but on the public road, every boy, every passing drove of sheep or cows, gives them a lift. Hence the incursion of a new weed is generally first noticed along the highway or the railroad. In Orange County I saw from the car window a field overrun with what I took to be the branching white mullein. Gray says it is found in Pennsylvania and at the head of Oneida Lake. Doubtless it had come by rail from one place or the other. Our botanist says of the bladder campion, a species of pink, that it has been naturalized around Boston; but it is now much farther west, and I know fields along the Hudson overrun with it. Streams and watercourses are the natural highway of the weeds. Some years ago, and by some means or other, the viper's bugloss, or blueweed, which is said to be a troublesome weed in Virginia, effected a lodgment near the head of the Esopus Creek, a tributary of the Hudson. From this point it has made its way down the stream, overrunning its banks and invading meadows and cultivated fields, and proving a serious obstacle to the farmer. All the gravelly, sandy margins and islands of the Esopus, sometimes acres in extent, are in June and July blue with it, and rye and oats and grass in the near fields find it a serious competitor for possession of the soil. It has gone down the Hudson, and is appearing in the fields along its shores. The tides carry it up the mouths of the streams where it takes root; the winds, or the birds, or other agencies, in time give it another lift, so that it is slowly but surely making its way inland. The bugloss belongs to what may be called beautiful weeds, despite its rough and bristly stalk. Its flowers are deep violet-blue, the stamens exserted, as the botanists say, that is, projected beyond the mouth of the corolla, with showy red anthers. This bit of red, mingling with the blue of the corolla, gives a very rich, warm purple hue to the flower, that is especially pleasing at a little distance. The best thing I know about this weed besides its good looks is that it yields honey or pollen to the bee.

Another foreign plant that the Esopus Creek has distributed along its shores and carried to the

Hudson is saponaria, known as "Bouncing Bet." It is a common and in places a troublesome weed in this valley. Bouncing Bet is, perhaps, its English name, as the pink-white complexion of its flowers with their perfume and the coarse, robust character of the plant really give it a kind of English feminine comeliness and bounce. It looks like a Yorkshire housemaid. Still another plant in my section, which I notice has been widely distributed by the agency of water, is the spiked loosestrife. It first appeared many years ago along the Wallkill; now it may be seen upon many of its tributaries and all along its banks; and in many of the marshy bays and coves along the Hudson, its great masses of purple-red bloom in middle and late summer affording a welcome relief to the traveler's eye. It also belongs to the class of beautiful weeds. It grows rank and tall, in dense communities, and always presents to the eye a generous mass of color. In places, the marshes and creek banks are all aglow with it, its wandlike spikes of flowers shooting up and uniting in volumes or pyramids of still flame. Its petals, when examined closely, present a curious wrinkled or crumpled appearance, like newly-washed linen; but when massed the effect is eminently pleasing. It also came from abroad, probably first brought to this country as a garden or ornamental plant.

As a curious illustration of how weeds are carried from one end of the earth to the other, Sir Joseph Hooker relates this circumstance: "On one occasion," he says, "landing on a small uninhabited island nearly at the Antipodes, the first evidence I met with of its having been previously visited by man was the English chickweed; and this I traced to a mound that marked the grave of a British sailor, and that was covered with the plant, doubtless the offspring of seed that had adhered to the spade or mattock with which the grave had been dug."

Ours is a weedy country because it is a roomy country. Weeds love a wide margin, and they find it here. You shall see more weeds in one day's travel in this country than in a week's journey in Europe. Our culture of the soil is not so close and thorough, our occupancy not so entire and exclusive. The weeds take up with the farmers' leavings, and find good fare. One may see a large slice taken from a field by elecampane, or by teasle or milkweed; whole acres given up to whiteweed, goldenrod, wild carrots, or the ox-eye daisy; meadows overrun with bear-weed, and sheep pastures nearly ruined by St. John's-wort or the Canada thistle. Our farms are so large and our husbandry so loose that we do not mind these things. By and by we shall clean them out. When Sir Joseph Hooker landed in New England a few years ago, he was surprised to find how the European plants flourished there. He found the wild chicory growing far more luxuriantly than he had ever seen it elsewhere, "forming a tangled mass of stems and branches, studded with turquoise-blue blossoms, and covering acres of ground." This is one of the many weeds that Emerson binds into a bouquet in his "Humble-Bee:"--

"Succory to match the sky, Columbine with horn of honey, Scented fern, and agrimony, Clover, catchfly, adder's tongue, And brier-roses, dwelt among."

A less accurate poet than Emerson would probably have let his reader infer that the bumblebee gathered honey from all these plants, but Emerson is careful to say only that she dwelt among them. Succory is one of Virgil's weeds also,--

"And spreading succ'ry chokes the rising field."

Is there not something in our soil and climate exceptionally favorable to weeds,--something harsh, ungenial, sharp-toothed, that is akin to them? How woody and rank and fibrous many varieties become, lasting the whole season, and standing up stark and stiff through the deep winter snows,--desiccated, preserved by our dry air! Do nettles and thistles bite so sharply in any other country? Let the farmer tell you how they bite of a dry midsummer day when he encounters them in his wheat or oat harvest.

Yet it is a fact that all our more pernicious weeds, like our vermin, are of Old World origin. They hold up their heads and assert themselves here, and take their fill of riot and license; they are avenged for their long years of repression by the stern hand of European agriculture. We have hardly a weed we can call our own. I recall but three that are at all noxious or troublesome, namely, milkweed, ragweed, and goldenrod; but who would miss the last from our fields and highways?

"Along the roadside, like the flowers of gold That tawny Incas for their gardens wrought, Heavy with sunshine droops the goldenrod,"sings Whittier. In Europe our goldenrod is cultivated in the flower gardens, as well it may be. The native species is found mainly in woods, and is much less showy than ours.

Our milkweed is tenacious of life; its roots lie deep, as if to get away from the plow, but it seldom infests cultivated crops. Then its stalk is so full of milk and its pod so full of silk that one cannot but ascribe good intentions to it, if it does sometimes overrun the meadow.

"In dusty pods the milkweed Its hidden silk has spun,"sings "H. H." in her "September".

Of our ragweed not much can be set down that is complimentary, except that its name in the botany is Ambrosia, food of the gods. It must be the food of the gods if anything, for, so far as I have observed, nothing terrestrial eats it, not even billy-goats. (Yet a correspondent writes me that in Kentucky the cattle eat it when hard-pressed, and that a certain old farmer there, one season when the hay crop failed, cut and harvested tons of it for his stock in winter. It is said that the milk and butter made from such hay is not at all suggestive of the traditional Ambrosia!) It is the bane of asthmatic patients, but the gardener makes short work of it. It is about the only one of our weeds that follows the plow and the harrow, and, except that it is easily destroyed, I should suspect it to be an immigrant from the Old World. Our fleabane is a troublesome weed at times, but good husbandry has little to dread from it.

But all the other outlaws of the farm and garden come to us from over seas; and what a long list it is:--

Common thistle, Gill, Canada thistle, Nightshade, Burdock, Buttercup, Yellow dock, Dandelion, Wild carrot, Wild mustard, Ox-eye daisy, Shepherd's purse, Chamomile, St. John's-wort, Mullein, Chickweed, Dead-nettle (Lamium), Purslane, Hemp-nettle (Galeopsis), Mallow, Elecampane,

Darnel, Plantain, Poison hemlock, Motherwort, Hop-clover, Stramonium, Yarrow, Catnip, Wild radish, Blue-weed, Wild parsnip, Stick-seed, Chicory, Hound's-tongue, Live-forever, Henbane, Toad-flax, Pigweed, Sheep-sorrel, Quitch grass, Mayweed,

and others less noxious. To offset this list we have given Europe the vilest of all weeds, a parasite that sucks up human blood, tobacco. Now if they catch the Colorado beetle of us, it will go far toward paying them off for the rats and the mice, and for other pests in our houses.

The more attractive and pretty of the British weeds--as the common daisy, of which the poets have made so much, the larkspur, which is a pretty cornfield weed, and the scarlet field-poppy, which flowers all summer, and is so taking amid the ripening grain--have not immigrated to our shores. Like a certain sweet rusticity and charm of European rural life, they do not thrive readily under our skies. Our fleabane has become a common roadside weed in England, and a few other of our native less-known plants have gained a foothold in the Old World. Our beautiful jewel-weed has recently appeared along certain of the English rivers.

Pokeweed is a native American, and what a lusty, royal plant it is! It never invades cultivated fields, but hovers about the borders and looks over the fences like a painted Indian sachem. Thoreau coveted its strong purple stalk for a cane, and the robins eat its dark crimson-juiced berries.

It is commonly believed that the mullein is indigenous to this country, for have we not heard that it is cultivated in European gardens, and christened the American velvet plant? Yet it, too, seems to have come over with the Pilgrims, and is most abundant in the older parts of the country. It abounds throughout Europe and Asia, and had its economic uses with the ancients. The Greeks made lamp-wicks of its dried leaves, and the Romans dipped its dried stalk in tallow for funeral torches. It affects dry uplands in this country, and, as it takes two years to mature, it is not a troublesome weed in cultivated crops. The first year it sits low upon the ground in its coarse flannel leaves, and makes ready; if the plow comes along now, its career is ended. The second season it starts upward its tall stalk, which in late summer is thickly set with small yellow flowers, and in fall is charged with myriads of fine black seeds. "As full as a dry mullein stalk of seeds" is almost equivalent to saying "as numerous as the sands upon the seashore."

Perhaps the most notable thing about the weeds that have come to us from the Old World, when compared with our native species, is their persistence, not to say pugnacity. They fight for the soil; they plant colonies here and there, and will not be rooted out. Our native weeds are for the most part shy and harmless, and retreat before cultivation, but the European outlaws follow man like vermin; they hang to his coat-skirts, his sheep transport them in their wool, his cow and horse in tail and mane. As I have before said, it is as with the rats and mice. The American rat is in the woods and is rarely seen even by woodmen, and the native mouse barely hovers upon the outskirts of civilization; while the Old World species defy our traps and our poison, and have usurped the land. So with the weeds. Take the thistle, for instance,--the common and abundant one everywhere, in fields and along highways, is the European species; while the native thistles, swamp thistle, pasture thistle, etc., are much more shy, and are not at all troublesome. The

Canada thistle, too, which came to us by way of Canada,--what a pest, what a usurper, what a defier of the plow and the harrow! I know of but one effectual way to treat it,--put on a pair of buckskin gloves, and pull up every plant that shows itself; this will effect a radical cure in two summers. Of course the plow or the scythe, if not allowed to rest more than a month at a time, will finally conquer it.

Or take the common St. John's-wort,--how has it established itself in our fields and become a most pernicious weed, very difficult to extirpate; while the native species are quite rare, and seldom or never invade cultivated fields, being found mostly in wet and rocky waste places. Of Old World origin, too, is the curled-leaf dock that is so annoying about one's garden and home meadows, its long tapering root clinging to the soil with such tenacity that I have pulled upon it till I could see stars without budging it; it has more lives than a cat, making a shift to live when pulled up and laid on top of the ground in the burning summer sun. Our native docks are mostly found in swamps, or near them, and are harmless.

Purslane--commonly called "pusley," and which has given rise to the saying, "as mean as pusley"--of course is not American. A good sample of our native purslane is the claytonia, or spring beauty, a shy, delicate plant that opens its rose-colored flowers in the moist, sunny places in the woods or along their borders so early in the season.

There are few more obnoxious weeds in cultivated ground than sheep-sorrel, also an Old World plant; while our native wood-sorrel,--belonging, it is true, to a different family of plants,--with its white, delicately veined flowers, or the variety with yellow flowers, is quite harmless. The same is true of the mallow, the vetch or tare, and other plants. We have no native plant so indestructible as garden orpine, or live-forever, which our grandmothers nursed and for which they are cursed by many a farmer. The fat, tender, succulent dooryard stripling turned out to be a monster that would devour the earth. I have seen acres of meadow land destroyed by it. The way to drown an amphibious animal is to never allow it to come to the surface to breathe, and this is the way to kill live-forever. It lives by its stalk and leaf, more than by its root, and, if cropped or bruised as soon as it comes to the surface, it will in time perish. It laughs the plow, the hoe, the cultivator to scorn, but grazing herds will eventually scotch it. Our two species of native orpine, Sedum ternatum and S. telephioides, are never troublesome as weeds.

The European weeds are sophisticated, domesticated, civilized; they have been to school to man for many hundred years, and they have learned to thrive upon him: their struggle for existence has been sharp and protracted; it has made them hardy and prolific; they will thrive in a lean soil, or they will wax strong in a rich one; in all cases they follow man and profit by him. Our native weeds, on the other hand, are furtive and retiring; they flee before the plow and the scythe, and hide in corners and remote waste places. Will they, too, in time, change their habits in this respect?

"Idle weeds are fast in growth," says Shakespeare, but that depends upon whether the competition is sharp and close. If the weed finds itself distanced, or pitted against great odds, it grows more slowly and is of diminished stature, but let it once get the upper hand and what strides it makes! Red-root will grow four or five feet high if it has a chance, or it will content itself with a few inches and mature its seed almost upon the ground.

Many of our worst weeds are plants that have escaped from cultivation, as the wild radish, which is troublesome in parts of New England; the wild carrot, which infests the fields in eastern New York; and live-forever, which thrives and multiplies under the plow and harrow. In my section an annoying weed is abutilon, or velvet-leaf, also called "old maid," which has fallen from the grace of the garden and followed the plow afield. It will manage to mature its seeds if not allowed to start till midsummer.

Of beautiful weeds quite a long list might be made without including any of the so-called wild flowers. A favorite of mine is the little moth mullein that blooms along the highway, and about the fields, and maybe upon the edge of the lawn, from midsummer till frost comes. In winter its slender stalk rises above the snow, bearing its round seed-pods on its pin-like stems, and is pleasing even then. Its flowers are yellow or white, large, wheel-shaped, and are borne vertically with filaments loaded with little tufts of violet wool. The plant has none of the coarse, hairy character of the common mullein. Our coneflower, which one of our poets has called the "brown-eyed daisy," has a pleasing effect when in vast numbers they invade a meadow (if it is not your meadow), their dark brown centres or disks and their golden rays showing conspicuously.

Bidens, two-teeth, or "pitchforks," as the boys call them, are welcomed by the eye when in late summer they make the swamps and wet waste places yellow with their blossoms.

Vervain is a beautiful weed, especially the blue or purple variety. Its drooping knotted threads also make a pretty etching upon the winter snow.

Iron-weed, which looks like an overgrown aster, has the same intense purple-blue color, and a royal profusion of flowers. There are giants among the weeds, as well as dwarfs and pigmies. One of the giants is purple eupatorium, which sometimes carries its corymbs of flesh-colored flowers ten and twelve feet high. A pretty and curious little weed, sometimes found growing in the edge of the garden, is the clasping specularia, a relative of the harebell and of the European Venus's looking-glass. Its leaves are shell-shaped, and clasp the stalk so as to form little shallow cups. In the bottom of each cup three buds appear that never expand into flowers; but when the top of the stalk is reached, one and sometimes two buds open a large, delicate purple-blue corolla. All the first-born of this plant are still-born, as it were; only the latest, which spring from its summit, attain to perfect bloom. A weed which one ruthlessly demolishes when he finds it hiding from the plow amid the strawberries, or under the currant-bushes and grapevines, is the dandelion; yet who would banish it from the meadows or the lawns, where it copies in gold upon the green expanse the stars of the midnight sky? After its first blooming comes its second and finer and more spiritual inflorescence, when its stalk, dropping its more earthly and carnal flower, shoots upward, and is presently crowned by a globe of the most delicate and aerial texture. It is like the poet's dream, which succeeds his rank and golden youth. This globe is a fleet of a hundred fairy balloons, each one of which bears a seed which it is destined to drop far from the parent source.

Most weeds have their uses; they are not wholly malevolent. Emerson says a weed is a plant whose virtues we have not yet discovered; but the wild creatures discover their virtues if we do not. The bumblebee has discovered that the hateful toad-flax, which nothing will eat, and which in some soils will run out the grass, has honey at its heart. Narrow-leaved plantain is readily eaten by cattle, and the honey-bee gathers much pollen from it. The ox-eye daisy makes a fair quality of hay if cut before it gets ripe. The cows will eat the leaves of the burdock and the stinging nettles of the woods. But what cannot a cow's tongue stand? She will crop the poison ivy with impunity, and I think would eat thistles if she found them growing in the garden. Leeks and garlics are readily eaten by cattle in the spring, and are said to be medicinal to them. Weeds that yield neither pasturage for bee nor herd, yet afford seeds to the fall and winter birds. This is true of most of the obnoxious weeds of the garden and of thistles. The wild lettuce yields down for the humming-bird's nest, and the flowers of whiteweed are used by the kingbird and cedar-bird.

Yet it is pleasant to remember that, in our climate, there are no weeds so persistent and lasting and universal as grass. Grass is the natural covering of the fields. There are but four weeds that I know of--milkweed, live-forever, Canada thistle, and toad-flax--that it will not run out in a good soil. We crop it and mow it year after year; and yet, if the season favors, it is sure to come again. Fields that have never known the plow, and never been seeded by man, are yet covered with grass. And in human nature, too, weeds are by no means in the ascendant, troublesome as they are. The good green grass of love and truthfulness and common sense is more universal, and crowds the idle weeds to the wall.

But weeds have this virtue: they are not easily discouraged; they never lose heart entirely; they die game. If they cannot have the best, they will take up with the poorest; if fortune is unkind to them to-day, they hope for better luck to-morrow; if they cannot lord it over a corn-hill, they will sit humbly at its foot and accept what comes; in all cases they make the most of their opportunities.

VII

AUTUMN TIDES

The season is always a little behind the sun in our climate, just as the tide is always a little behind the moon. According to the calendar, the summer ought to culminate about the 21st of June, but in reality it is some weeks later; June is a maiden month all through. It is not high noon in nature till about the first or second week in July. When the chestnut-tree blooms, the meridian of the year is reached. By the first of August it is fairly one o'clock. The lustre of the season begins to dim, the foliage of the trees and woods to tarnish, the plumage of the birds to fade, and their songs to cease. The hints of approaching fall are on every hand. How suggestive this thistle-down, for instance, which, as I sit by the open window, comes in and brushes softly across my hand! The first snowflake tells of winter not more plainly than this driving down heralds the approach of fall. Come here, my fairy, and tell me whence you come and whither you go? What brings you to port here, you gossamer ship sailing the great sea? How exquisitely frail and delicate! One of the lightest things in nature; so light that in the closed room here it will hardly rest in my open palm. A feather is a clod beside it. Only a spider's web will hold it; coarser objects have no power over it. Caught in the upper currents of the air and rising above the clouds, it might sail perpetually. Indeed, one fancies it might almost traverse the interstellar ether and drive against the stars. And every thistle-head by the roadside holds hundreds of these sky rovers,--imprisoned Ariels unable to set themselves free. Their liberation may be by the shock of the wind, or the rude contact of cattle, but it is oftener the work of the goldfinch with its complaining brood. The seed of the thistle is the proper food of this bird, and in obtaining it myriads of these winged creatures are scattered to the breeze. Each one is fraught with a seed which it exists to sow, but its wild careering and soaring does not fairly begin till its burden is dropped, and its spheral form is complete. The seeds of many plants and trees are disseminated through the agency of birds; but the thistle furnishes its own birds,--flocks of them, with wings more ethereal and tireless than were ever given to mortal creature. From the pains Nature thus takes to sow the thistle broadcast over the land, it might be expected to be one of the most troublesome and abundant of weeds. But such is not the case; the more pernicious and baffling weeds, like snapdragon or blind nettles, being more local and restricted in their habits, and unable to fly at all.

[Illustration: AMONG THE ROCKS]

In the fall the battles of the spring are fought over again, beginning at the other or little end of the series. There is the same advance and retreat, with many feints and alarms, between the contending forces, that was witnessed in April and May. The spring comes like a tide running against a strong wind; it is ever beaten back, but ever gaining ground, with now and then a mad "push upon the land" as if to overcome its antagonist at one blow. The cold from the north encroaches upon us in about the same fashion. In September or early in October it usually makes a big stride forward and blackens all the more delicate plants, and hastens the "mortal ripening" of the foliage of the trees, but it is presently beaten back again, and the genial warmth repossesses the land. Before long, however, the cold returns to the charge with augmented forces and gains much ground.

The course of the seasons never does run smooth, owing to the unequal distribution of land and water, mountain, wood, and plain.

An equilibrium, however, is usually reached in our climate in October, sometimes the most marked in November, forming the delicious Indian summer; a truce is declared, and both forces, heat and cold, meet and mingle in friendly converse on the field. In the earlier season, this poise of the temperature, this slack-water in nature, comes in May and June; but the October calm is most marked. Day after day, and sometimes week after week, you cannot tell which way the current is setting. Indeed, there is no current, but the season seems to drift a little this way or a little that, just as the breeze happens to freshen a little in one quarter or the other. The fall of '74 was the most remarkable in this respect I remember ever to have seen. The equilibrium of the season lasted from the middle of October till near December, with scarcely a break. There were six weeks of Indian summer, all gold by day, and, when the moon came, all silver by night. The river was so smooth at times as to be almost invisible, and in its place was the indefinite continuation of the opposite shore down toward the nether world. One seemed to be in an enchanted land and to breathe all day the atmosphere of fable and romance. Not a smoke, but a kind of shining nimbus filled all the spaces. The vessels would drift by as if in mid-air with all their sails set. The gypsy blood in one, as Lowell calls it, could hardly stay between four walls and see such days go by. Living in tents, in groves and on the hills, seemed the only natural life.

Late in December we had glimpses of the same weather,--the earth had not yet passed all the golden isles. On the 27th of that month, I find I made this entry in my note-book: "A soft, hazy day, the year asleep and dreaming of the Indian summer again. Not a breath of air and not a ripple on the river. The sunshine is hot as it falls across my table."

But what a terrible winter followed! what a savage chief the fair Indian maiden gave birth to!

This halcyon period of our autumn will always in some way be associated with the Indian. It is red and yellow and dusky like him. The smoke of his camp-fire seems again in the air. The memory of him pervades the woods. His plumes and moccasins and blanket of skins form just the costume the season demands. It was doubtless his chosen period. The gods smiled upon him then if ever. The time of the chase, the season of the buck and the doe, and of the ripening of all forest fruits; the time when all men are incipient hunters, when the first frosts have given pungency to the air, when to be abroad on the hills or in the woods is a delight that both old and young feel,--if the red aborigine ever had his summer of fullness and contentment, it must have been at this season, and it fitly bears his name.

In how many respects fall imitates or parodies the spring! It is indeed, in some of its features, a sort of second youth of the year. Things emerge and become conspicuous again. The trees attract all eyes as in May. The birds come forth from their summer privacy and parody their spring reunions and rivalries; some of them sing a little after a silence of months. The robins, blue-birds, meadow-larks, sparrows, crows, all sport, and call, and behave in a manner suggestive of spring. The cock grouse drums in the woods as he did in April and May. The pigeons reappear, and the wild geese and ducks. The witch-hazel blooms. The trout spawns. The streams are again full. The air is humid, and the moisture rises in the ground. Nature is breaking camp, as in spring she was going into camp. The spring yearning and restlessness is represented in one by the increased desire to travel.

Spring is the inspiration, fall the expiration. Both seasons have their equinoxes, both their filmy, hazy air, their ruddy forest tints, their cold rains, their drenching fogs, their mystic moons; both have the same solar light and warmth, the same rays of the sun; yet, after all, how different the feelings which they inspire! One is the morning, the other the evening; one is youth, the other is age.

The difference is not merely in us; there is a subtle difference in the air, and in the influences that emanate upon us from the dumb forms of nature. All the senses report a difference. The sun seems to have burned out. One recalls the notion of Herodotus that he is grown feeble, and retreats to the south because he can no longer face the cold and the storms from the north. There is a growing potency about his beams in spring, a waning splendor about them in fall. One is the kindling fire, the other the subsiding flame.

It is rarely that an artist succeeds in painting unmistakably the difference between sunrise and sunset; and it is equally a trial of his skill to put upon canvas the difference between early spring and late fall, say between April and November. It was long ago observed that the shadows are more opaque in the morning than in the evening; the struggle between the light and the darkness more marked, the gloom more solid, the contrasts more sharp, etc. The rays of the morning sun chisel out and cut down the shadows in a way those of the setting sun do not. Then the sunlight is whiter and newer in the morning,--not so yellow and diffused. A difference akin to this is true of the two seasons I am speaking of. The spring is the morning sunlight, clear and determined; the autumn, the afternoon rays, pensive, lessening, golden.

Does not the human frame yield to and sympathize with the seasons? Are there not more births in the spring and more deaths in the fall? In the spring one vegetates; his thoughts turn to sap; another kind of activity seizes him; he makes new wood which does not harden till past midsummer. For my part, I find all literary work irksome from April to August; my sympathies run in other channels; the grass grows where meditation walked. As fall approaches, the currents mount to the head again. But my thoughts do not ripen well till after there has been a frost. The burrs will not open much before that. A man's thinking, I take it, is a kind of combustion, as is the ripening of fruits and leaves, and he wants plenty of oxygen in the air.

Then the earth seems to have become a positive magnet in the fall; the forge and anvil of the sun have had their effect. In the spring it is negative to all intellectual conditions, and drains one of his lightning.

To-day, October 21st, I found the air in the bushy fields and lanes under the woods loaded with the perfume of the witch-hazel,--a sweetish, sickening odor. With the blooming of this bush, Nature says, "Positively the last." It is a kind of birth in death, of spring in fall, that impresses one as a little uncanny. All trees and shrubs form their flower-buds in the fall, and keep the secret till spring. How comes the witch-hazel to be the one exception, and to celebrate its floral nuptials on the funeral day of its foliage? No doubt it will be found that the spirit of some lovelorn squaw has passed into this bush, and that this is why it blooms in the Indian summer rather than in the white man's spring.

But it makes the floral series of the woods complete. Between it and the shad-blow of earliest spring lies the mountain of bloom; the latter at the base on one side, this at the base on the other, with the chestnut blossoms at the top in midsummer.

A peculiar feature of our fall may sometimes be seen of a clear afternoon late in the season. Looking athwart the fields under the sinking sun, the ground appears covered with a shining veil of gossamer. A fairy net, invisible at midday and which the position of the sun now reveals, rests upon the stubble and upon the spears of grass covering acres in extent,--the work of innumerable little spiders. The cattle walk through it, but do not seem to break it. Perhaps a fly would make his mark upon it. At the same time, stretching from the tops of the trees, or from the top of a stake in the fence, and leading off toward the sky, may be seen the cables of the flying spider,--a fairy bridge from the visible to the invisible. Occasionally seen against a deep mass of shadow, and perhaps enlarged by clinging particles of dust, they show quite plainly and sag down like a stretched rope, or sway and undulate like a hawser in the tide.

They recall a verse of our rugged poet, Walt Whitman:--

"A noiseless patient spider, I mark'd where, in a little promontory, it stood isolated: Mark'd how, to explore the vacant, vast surrounding, It launch'd forth filament, filament, filament out of itself; Ever unreeling them--ever tirelessly spreading them.

"And you, O my soul, where you stand, Surrounded, surrounded, in measureless oceans of space, Ceaselessly musing, venturing, throwing,-- Seeking the spheres to connect them; Till the bridge you will need be formed--till the ductile anchor hold; Till the gossamer thread you fling, catch somewhere, O my soul."

To return a little, September may be described as the month of tall weeds. Where they have been suffered to stand, along fences, by roadsides, and in forgotten corners,--redroot, pigweed, ragweed, vervain, goldenrod, burdock, elecampane, thistles, teasels, nettles, asters, etc.,--how they lift themselves up as if not afraid to be seen now! They are all outlaws; every man's hand is against them; yet how surely they hold their own! They love the roadside, because here they are comparatively safe; and ragged and dusty, like the common tramps that they are, they form one of the characteristic features of early fall.

I have often noticed in what haste certain weeds are at times to produce their seeds. Redroot will grow three or four feet high when it has the whole season before it; but let it get a late start, let it come up in August, and it scarcely gets above the ground before it heads out, and apparently goes to work with all its might and main to mature its seed. In the growth of most plants or weeds, April and May represent their root, June and July their stalk, and August and September their flower and seed. Hence, when the stalk months are stricken out, as in the present case, there is only time for a shallow root and a foreshortened head. I think most weeds that get a late start show this curtailment of stalk, and this solicitude to reproduce themselves. But I have not observed that any of the cereals are so worldly wise. They have not had to think and shift for themselves as the weeds have. It does indeed look like a kind of forethought in the redroot. It is killed by the first frost, and hence knows the danger of delay.

How rich in color, before the big show of the tree foliage has commenced, our roadsides are in places in early autumn,--rich to the eye that goes hurriedly by and does not look too closely,-- with the profusion of goldenrod and blue and purple asters dashed in upon here and there with the crimson leaves of the dwarf sumac; and at intervals, rising out of the fence corner or crowning a ledge of rocks, the dark green of the cedars with the still fire of the woodbine at its heart. I wonder if the waysides of other lands present any analogous spectacles at this season.

Then, when the maples have burst out into color, showing like great bonfires along the hills, there is indeed a feast for the eye. A maple before your windows in October, when the sun shines upon it, will make up for a good deal of the light it has excluded; it fills the room with a soft golden glow.

Thoreau, I believe, was the first to remark upon the individuality of trees of the same species with respect to their foliage,--some maples ripening their leaves early and some late, and some being of one tint and some of another; and, moreover, that each tree held to the same characteristics, year after year. There is, indeed, as great a variety among the maples as among the trees of an apple orchard; some are harvest apples, some are fall apples, and some are winter apples, each with a tint of its own. Those late ripeners are the winter varieties,--the Rhode Island greenings or swaars of their kind. The red maple is the early astrachan. Then come the red-streak, the yellow-sweet, and others. There are windfalls among them, too, as among the apples, and one side or hemisphere of the leaf is usually brighter than the other.

The ash has been less noticed for its autumnal foliage than it deserves. The richest shades of plum color to be seen--becoming by and by, or in certain lights, a deep maroon--are afforded by this tree. Then at a distance there seems to be a sort of bloom on it, as upon the grape or plum. Amid a grove of yellow maple, it makes a most pleasing contrast.

By mid-October, most of the Rip Van Winkles among our brute creatures have lain down for their winter nap. The toads and turtles have buried themselves in the earth. The woodchuck is in his hibernaculum, the skunk in his, the mole in his; and the black bear has his selected, and will go in when the snow comes. He does not like the looks of his big tracks in the snow. They publish his goings and comings too plainly. The coon retires about the same time. The provident wood-mice and the chipmunk are laying by a winter supply of nuts or grain, the former usually in decayed trees, the latter in the ground. I have observed that any unusual disturbance in the woods, near where the chipmunk has his den, will cause him to shift his quarters. One October, for many successive days, I saw one carrying into his hole buckwheat which he had stolen from a near field. The hole was only a few rods from where we were getting out stone, and as our work progressed, and the racket and uproar increased, the chipmunk became alarmed. He ceased carrying in, and after much hesitating and darting about, and some prolonged absences, he began to carry out; he had determined to move; if the mountain fell, he, at least, would be away in time. So, by mouthfuls or cheekfuls, the grain was transferred to a new place. He did not make a "bee" to get it done, but carried it all himself, occupying several days, and making a trip about every ten minutes.

The red and gray squirrels do not lay by winter stores; their cheeks are made without pockets, and whatever they transport is carried in the teeth. They are more or less active all winter, but October and November are their festal months. Invade some butternut or hickory-nut grove on a frosty October morning, and hear the red squirrel beat the "juba" on a horizontal branch. It is a most lively jig, what the boys call a "regular break-down," interspersed with squeals and snickers and derisive laughter. The most noticeable peculiarity about the vocal part of it is the fact that it is a kind of duet. In other words, by some ventriloquial tricks, he appears to accompany himself, as if his voice split up, a part forming a low guttural sound, and a part a shrill nasal sound.

The distant bark of the more wary gray squirrel may be heard about the same time. There is a teasing and ironical tone in it also, but the gray squirrel is not the Puck the red is.

Insects also go into winter-quarters by or before this time; the bumblebee, hornet, and wasp. But here only royalty escapes: the queen-mother alone foresees the night of winter coming and the morning of spring beyond. The rest of the tribe try gypsying for a while, but perish in the first frosts. The present October I surprised the queen of the yellow-jackets in the woods looking out a suitable retreat. The royal dame was house-hunting, and, on being disturbed by my inquisitive poking among the leaves, she got up and flew away with a slow, deep hum. Her body was unusually distended, whether with fat or eggs I am unable to say. In September I took down the nest of the black hornet and found several large queens in it, but the workers had all gone. The queens were evidently weathering the first frosts and storms here, and waiting for the Indian summer to go forth and seek a permanent winter abode. If the covers could be taken off the fields and woods at this season, how many interesting facts of natural history would be revealed!--the crickets, ants, bees, reptiles, animals, and, for aught I know, the spiders and flies asleep or getting ready to sleep in their winter dormitories; the fires of life banked up, and burning just enough to keep the spark over till spring.

The fish all run down the stream in the fall except the trout; it runs up or stays up and spawns in November, the male becoming as brilliantly tinted as the deepest-dyed maple leaf. I have often wondered why the trout spawns in the fall, instead of in the spring like other fish. Is it not because a full supply of clear spring water can be counted on at that season more than at any other? The brooks are not so liable to be suddenly muddied by heavy showers, and defiled with the washings of the roads and fields, as they are in spring and summer. The artificial breeder finds that absolute purity of water is necessary to hatch the spawn; also that shade and a low temperature are indispensable.

Our Northern November day itself is like spring water. It is melted frost, dissolved snow. There is a chill in it and an exhilaration also. The forenoon is all morning and the afternoon all evening. The shadows seem to come forth and to revenge themselves upon the day. The sunlight is diluted with darkness. The colors fade from the landscape, and only the sheen of the river lights up the gray and brown distance.

VIII

A SHARP LOOKOUT

One has only to sit down in the woods or fields, or by the shore of the river or lake, and nearly everything of interest will come round to him,--the birds, the animals, the insects; and presently, after his eye has got accustomed to the place, and to the light and shade, he will probably see some plant or flower that he had sought in vain for, and that is a pleasant surprise to him. So, on a large scale, the student and lover of nature has this advantage over people who gad up and down the world, seeking some novelty or excitement; he has only to stay at home and see the procession pass. The great globe swings around to him like a revolving showcase; the change of the seasons is like the passage of strange and new countries; the zones of the earth, with all their beauties and marvels, pass one's door and linger long in the passing. What a voyage is this we make without leaving for a night our own fireside! St. Pierre well says that a sense of the power and mystery of nature shall spring up as fully in one's heart after he has made the circuit of his own field as after returning from a voyage round the world. I sit here amid the junipers of the Hudson, with purpose every year to go to Florida, or to the West Indies, or to the Pacific coast, yet the seasons pass and I am still loitering, with a half-defined suspicion, perhaps, that, if I remain quiet and keep a sharp lookout, these countries will come to me. I may stick it out yet, and not miss much after all. The great trouble is for Mohammed to know when the mountain really comes to him. Sometimes a rabbit or a jay or a little warbler brings the woods to my door. A loon on the river, and the Canada lakes are here; the sea-gulls and the fish hawk bring the sea; the call of the wild gander at night, what does it suggest? and the eagle flapping by, or floating along on a raft of ice, does not he bring the mountain? One spring morning five swans flew above my barn in single file, going northward,--an express train bound for Labrador. It was a more exhilarating sight than if I had seen them in their native haunts. They made a breeze in my mind, like a noble passage in a poem. How gently their great wings flapped; how easy to fly when spring gives the impulse! On another occasion I saw a line of fowls, probably swans, going northward, at such a height that they appeared like a faint, waving black line against the sky. They must have been at an altitude of two or three miles. I was looking intently at the clouds to see which way they moved, when the birds came into my field of vision. I should never have seen them had they not crossed the precise spot upon which my eye was fixed. As it was near sundown, they were probably launched for an all-night pull. They were going with great speed, and as they swayed a little this way and that, they suggested a slender, all but invisible, aerial serpent cleaving the ether. What a highway was pointed out up there!--an easy grade from the Gulf to Hudson's Bay.

Then the typical spring and summer and autumn days, of all shades and complexions,--one cannot afford to miss any of them; and when looked out upon from one's own spot of earth, how much more beautiful and significant they are! Nature comes home to one most when he is at home; the stranger and traveler finds her a stranger and a traveler also. One's own landscape comes in time to be a sort of outlying part of himself; he has sowed himself broadcast upon it, and it reflects his own moods and feelings; he is sensitive to the verge of the horizon: cut those trees, and he bleeds; mar those hills, and he suffers. How has the farmer planted himself in his fields; builded himself into his stone walls, and evoked the sympathy of the hills by his struggle! This home feeling, this domestication of nature, is important to the observer. This is the bird-lime with which he catches the bird; this is the private door that admits him behind the scenes. This is one source of Gilbert White's charm, and of the charm of Thoreau's "Walden."

The birds that come about one's door in winter, or that build in his trees in summer, what a peculiar interest they have! What crop have I sowed in Florida or in California, that I should go there to reap? I should be only a visitor, or formal caller upon nature, and the family would all wear masks. No; the place to observe nature is where you are; the walk to take to-day is the walk you took yesterday. You will not find just the same things: both the observed and the observer have changed; the ship is on another tack in both cases.

I shall probably never see another just such day as yesterday was, because one can never exactly repeat his observation,--cannot turn the leaf of the book of life backward,--and because each day has characteristics of its own. This was a typical March day, clear, dry, hard, and windy, the river rumpled and crumpled, the sky intense, distant objects strangely near; a day full of strong light, unusual; an extraordinary lightness and clearness all around the horizon, as if there were a diurnal aurora streaming up and burning through the sunlight; smoke from the first spring fires rising up in various directions,--a day that winnowed the air, and left no film in the sky. At night, how the big March bellows did work! Venus was like a great lamp in the sky. The stars all seemed brighter than usual, as if the wind blew them up like burning coals. Venus actually seemed to flare in the wind.

Each day foretells the next, if one could read the signs; to-day is the progenitor of to-morrow. When the atmosphere is telescopic, and distant objects stand out unusually clear and sharp, a storm is near. We are on the crest of the wave, and the depression follows quickly. It often happens that clouds are not so indicative of a storm as the total absence of clouds. In this state of the atmosphere the stars are unusually numerous and bright at night, which is also a bad omen.

I find this observation confirmed by Humboldt. "It appears," he says, "that the transparency of the air is prodigiously increased when a certain quantity of water is uniformly diffused through it." Again, he says that the mountaineers of the Alps "predict a change of weather when, the air being calm, the Alps covered with perpetual snow seem on a sudden to be nearer the observer, and their outlines are marked with great distinctness on the azure sky." He further observes that the same condition of the atmosphere renders distant sounds more audible.

There is one redness in the east in the morning that means storm, another that means wind. The former is broad, deep, and angry; the clouds look like a huge bed of burning coals just raked open; the latter is softer, more vapory, and more widely extended. Just at the point where the sun is going to rise, and some minutes in advance of his coming, there sometimes rises straight upward a rosy column; it is like a shaft of deeply dyed vapor, blending with and yet partly separated from the clouds, and the base of which presently comes to glow like the sun itself. The day that follows is pretty certain to be very windy. At other times the under sides of the eastern clouds are all turned to pink or rose-colored wool; the transformation extends until nearly the whole sky flushes, even the west glowing slightly; the sign is always to be interpreted as meaning fair weather.

The approach of great storms is seldom heralded by any striking or unusual phenomenon. The real weather gods are free from brag and bluster; but the sham gods fill the sky with portentous signs and omens. I recall one 5th of March as a day that would have filled the ancient observers with dreadful forebodings. At ten o'clock the sun was attended by four extraordinary sun-dogs. A large bright halo encompassed him, on the top of which the segment of a larger circle rested, forming a sort of heavy brilliant crown. At the bottom of the circle, and depending from it, was a mass of soft, glowing, iridescent vapor. On either side, like fragments of the larger circle, were two brilliant arcs. Altogether, it was the most portentous storm-breeding sun I ever beheld. In a dark hemlock wood in a valley, the owls were hooting ominously, and the crows dismally cawing. Before night the storm set in, a little sleet and rain of a few hours' duration, insignificant enough compared with the signs and wonders that preceded it.

To what extent the birds or animals can foretell the weather is uncertain. When the swallows are seen hawking very high it is a good indication; the insects upon which they feed venture up there only in the most auspicious weather. Yet bees will continue to leave the hive when a storm is imminent. I am told that one of the most reliable weather signs they have down in Texas is afforded by the ants. The ants bring their eggs up out of their underground retreats, and expose them to the warmth of the sun to be hatched. When they are seen carrying them in again in great haste, though there be not a cloud in the sky, your walk or your drive must be postponed: a storm is at hand. There is a passage in Virgil that is doubtless intended to embody a similar observation, though none of his translators seem to have hit its meaning accurately:--

"S � ius et tectis penetralibus extulit ova Angustum formica terens iter:"

"Often also has the pismire making a narrow road brought forth her eggs out of the hidden recesses" is the literal translation of old John Martyn.

"Also the ant, incessantly traveling The same straight way with the eggs of her hidden store,"

is one of the latest metrical translations. Dryden has it:--

"The careful ant her secret cell forsakes And drags her eggs along the narrow tracks,"

which comes nearer to the fact. When a storm is coming, Virgil also makes his swallows skim low about the lake, which agrees with the observation above.

The critical moments of the day as regards the weather are at sunrise and sunset A clear sunset is always a good sign; an obscured sun, just at the moment of going down after a bright day, bodes storm. There is much truth, too, in the saying that if it rain before seven, it will clear before eleven. Nine times in ten it will turn out thus. The best time for it to begin to rain or snow, if it wants to hold out, is about mid-forenoon. The great storms usually begin at this time. On all occasions the weather is very sure to declare itself before eleven o'clock. If you are going on a picnic, or are going to start on a journey, and the morning is unsettled, wait till ten and one half o'clock, and you shall know what the remainder of the day will be. Midday clouds and afternoon clouds, except in the season of thunderstorms, are usually harmless idlers and vagabonds. But more to be relied on than any obvious sign is that subtle perception of the condition of the weather which a man has who spends much of his time in the open air. He can hardly tell how he knows it is going to rain; he hits the fact as an Indian does the mark with his arrow, without calculating and by a kind of sure instinct. As you read a man's purpose in his face, so you learn to read the purpose of the weather in the face of the day.

In observing the weather, however, as in the diagnosis of disease, the diathesis is all-important. All signs fail in a drought, because the predisposition, the diathesis, is so strongly toward fair weather; and the opposite signs fail during a wet spell, because nature is caught in the other rut.

Observe the lilies of the field. Sir John Lubbock says the dandelion lowers itself after flowering, and lies close to the ground while it is maturing its seed, and then rises up. It is true that the dandelion lowers itself after flowering, retires from society, as it were, and meditates in seclusion; but after it lifts itself up again the stalk begins anew to grow, it lengthens daily, keeping just above the grass till the fruit is ripened, and the little globe of silvery down is carried many inches higher than was the ring of golden flowers. And the reason is obvious. The plant depends upon the wind to scatter its seeds; every one of these little vessels spreads a sail to the breeze, and it is necessary that they be launched above the grass and weeds, amid which they would be caught and held did the stalk not continue to grow and outstrip the rival vegetation. It is a curious instance of foresight in a weed.

I wish I could read as clearly this puzzle of the button-balls (American plane-tree). Why has Nature taken such particular pains to keep these balls hanging to the parent tree intact till spring? What secret of hers has she buttoned in so securely? for these buttons will not come off. The wind cannot twist them off, nor warm nor wet hasten or retard them. The stem, or peduncle, by which the ball is held in the fall and winter, breaks up into a dozen or more threads or strands, that are stronger than those of hemp. When twisted tightly they make a little cord that I find it impossible to break with my hands. Had they been longer, the Indian would surely have used them to make his bow-strings and all the other strings he required. One could hang himself with a small cord of them. (In South America, Humboldt saw excellent cordage made by the Indians from the petioles of the Chiquichiqui palm.) Nature has determined that these buttons should stay on. In order that the seeds of this tree may germinate, it is probably necessary that they be kept dry during the winter, and reach the ground after the season of warmth and moisture is fully established. In May, just as the leaves and the new balls are emerging, at the touch of a warm, moist south wind, these spherical packages suddenly go to pieces--explode, in fact, like tiny bombshells that were fused to carry to this point--and scatter their seeds to the four winds. They yield at the same time a fine pollen-like dust that one would suspect played some part in fertilizing the new balls, did not botany teach him otherwise. At any rate, it is the only deciduous tree I know of that does not let go the old seed till the new is well on the way. It is plain why the sugar-berry-tree or lotus holds its drupes all winter: it is in order that the birds may come and sow the seed. The berries are like small gravel stones with a sugar coating, and a bird will not eat them till he is pretty hard pressed, but in late fall and winter the robins, cedar-birds, and bluebirds devour them readily, and of course lend their wings to scatter the seed far and wide. The same is true of juniper-berries, and the fruit of the bitter-sweet.

In certain other cases where the fruit tends to hang on during the winter, as with the bladder-nut and the honey-locust, it is probably because the frost and the perpetual moisture of the ground would rot or kill the germ. To beechnuts, chestnuts, and acorns the moisture of the ground and the covering of leaves seem congenial, though too much warmth and moisture often cause the acorns to germinate prematurely. I have found the ground under the oaks in December covered with nuts, all anchored to the earth by purple sprouts. But the winter which follows such untimely growths generally proves fatal to them.

One must always cross-question nature if he would get at the truth, and he will not get at it then unless he frames his questions with great skill. Most persons are unreliable observers because they put only leading questions, or vague questions.

Perhaps there is nothing in the operations of nature to which we can properly apply the term intelligence, yet there are many things that at first sight look like it. Place a tree or plant in an unusual position and it will prove itself equal to the occasion, and behave in an unusual manner; it will show original resources; it will seem to try intelligently to master the difficulties. Up by Furlow Lake, where I was camping out, a young hemlock had become established upon the end of a large and partly decayed log that reached many feet out into the lake. The young tree was eight or nine feet high; it had sent its roots down into the log and clasped it around on the outside, and had apparently discovered that there was water instead of soil immediately beneath it, and that its sustenance must be sought elsewhere and that quickly. Accordingly it had started one large root, by far the largest of all, for the shore along the top of the log. This root, when I saw the tree, was six or seven feet long, and had bridged more than half the distance that separated the tree from the land.

Was this a kind of intelligence? If the shore had lain in the other direction, no doubt at all but the root would have started for the other side. I know a yellow pine that stands on the side of a steep hill. To make its position more secure, it has thrown out a large root at right angles with its stem directly into the bank above it, which acts as a stay or guy-rope. It was positively the best thing the tree could do. The earth has washed away so that the root where it leaves the tree is two feet above the surface of the soil.

Yet both these cases are easily explained, and without attributing any power of choice, or act of intelligent selection, to the trees. In the case of the little hemlock upon the partly submerged log, roots were probably thrown out equally in all directions; on all sides but one they reached the water and stopped growing; the water checked them; but on the land side, the root on the top of the log, not meeting with any obstacle of the kind, kept on growing, and thus pushing its way toward the shore. It was a case of survival, not of the fittest, but of that which the situation favored,--the fittest with reference to position.

So with the pine-tree on the side of the hill. It probably started its roots in all directions, but only the one on the upper side survived and matured. Those on the lower side finally perished, and others lower down took their places. Thus the whole life upon the globe, as we see it, is the result of this blind groping and putting forth of Nature in every direction, with failure of some of her ventures and the success of others, the circumstances, the environments, supplying the checks and supplying the stimulus, the seed falling upon the barren places just the same as upon the fertile. No discrimination on the part of Nature that we can express in the terms of our own consciousness, but ceaseless experiments in every possible direction. The only thing inexplicable is the inherent impulse to experiment, the original push, the principle of Life.

The good observer of nature holds his eye long and firmly to the point, as one does when looking at a puzzle picture, and will not be baffled. The cat catches the mouse, not merely because she watches for him, but because she is armed to catch him and is quick. So the observer finally gets the fact, not only because he has patience, but because his eye is sharp and his inference swift. Many a shrewd old farmer looks upon the milky way as a kind of weathercock, and will tell you that the way it points at night indicates the direction of the wind the following day. So, also, every new moon is either a dry moon or a wet moon, dry if a powder-horn would hang upon the lower limb, wet if it would not; forgetting the fact that, as a rule, when it is dry in one, part of the continent it is wet in some other part, and vice versa. When he kills his hogs in the fall, if the pork be very hard and solid he predicts a severe winter; if soft and loose, the opposite; again overlooking the fact that the kind of food and the temperature of the fall make the pork hard or make it soft. So with a hundred other signs, all the result of hasty and incomplete observations.

One season, the last day of December was very warm. The bees were out of the hive, and there was no frost in the air or in the ground. I was walking in the woods, when as I paused in the shade of a hemlock-tree I heard a sound proceed from beneath the wet leaves on the ground but a few feet from me that suggested a frog. Following it cautiously up, I at last determined upon the exact spot from whence the sound issued; lifting up the thick layer of leaves, there sat a frog--the wood frog, one of the first to appear in the marshes in spring, and which I have elsewhere called the "clucking frog"--in a little excavation in the surface of the leaf-mould. As it sat there the top of its back was level with the surface of the ground. This, then, was its hibernaculum; here it was prepared to pass the winter, with only a coverlid of wet matted leaves between it and zero weather. Forthwith I set up as a prophet of warm weather, and among other things predicted a failure of the ice crop on the river; which, indeed, others, who had not heard frogs croak on the 31st of December, had also begun to predict. Surely, I thought, this frog knows what it is about; here is the wisdom of nature; it would have gone deeper into the ground than that if a severe winter was approaching; so I was not anxious about my coal-bin, nor disturbed by longings for Florida. But what a winter followed, the winter of 1885, when the Hudson became coated with ice nearly two feet thick, and when March was as cold as January! I thought of my frog under the hemlock and wondered how it was faring. So one day the latter part of March, when the snow was gone, and there was a feeling of spring in the air, I turned aside in my walk to investigate it. The matted leaves were still frozen hard, but I succeeded in lifting them up and exposing the frog. There it sat as fresh and unscathed as in the fall. The ground beneath and all about it was still frozen like a rock, but apparently it had some means of its own of resisting the frost. It winked and bowed its head when I touched it, but did not seem inclined to leave its retreat. Some days later, after the frost was nearly all out of the ground, I passed that way, and found my frog had come out of its seclusion, and was resting amid the dry leaves. There was not much jump in it yet, but its color was growing lighter. A few more warm days, and its fellows, and doubtless itself too, were croaking and gamboling in the marshes.

This incident convinced me of two things; namely, that frogs know no more about the coming weather than we do, and that they do not retreat as deep into the ground to pass the winter as has been supposed. I used to think the muskrats could foretell an early and a severe winter, and have so written. But I am now convinced they cannot; they know as little about it as I do. Sometimes on an early and severe frost they seem to get alarmed and go to building their houses, but usually they seem to build early or late, high or low, just as the whim takes them.

In most of the operations of nature there is at least one unknown quantity; to find the exact value of this unknown factor is not so easy. The wool of the sheep, the fur of the animals, the feathers of the fowls, the husks of the maize, why are they thicker some seasons than others; what is the value of the unknown quantity her? Does it indicate a severe winter approaching? Only observations extending over a series of years could determine the point. How much patient observation it takes to settle many of the facts in the lives of the birds, animals, and insects! Gilbert White was all his life trying to determine whether or not swallows passed the winter in a torpid state in the mud at the bottom of ponds and marshes, and he died ignorant of the truth that they do not. Do honey-bees injure the grape and other fruits by puncturing the skin for the juice? The most patient watching by many skilled eyes all over the country has not yet settled the point. For my own part, I am convinced that they do not. The honey-bee is not the rough-and-ready freebooter that the wasp and bumblebee are; she has somewhat of feminine timidity, and leaves the first rude assaults to them. I knew the honey-bee was very fond of the locust blossoms, and that the trees hummed like a hive in the height of their flowering, but I did not know that the bumblebee was ever the sapper and miner that went ahead in this enterprise, till one day I placed myself amid the foliage of a locust and saw him savagely bite through the shank of the flower and extract the nectar, followed by a honey-bee that in every instance searched for this opening, and probed long and carefully for the leavings of her burly purveyor. The bumblebee rifles the dicentra and the columbine of their treasures in the same manner, namely, by slitting their pockets from the outside, and the honey-bee gleans after him, taking the small change he leaves. In the case of the locust, however, she usually obtains the honey without the aid of the larger bee.

Speaking of the honey-bee reminds me that the subtle and sleight-of-hand manner in which she fills her baskets with pollen and propolis is characteristic of much of Nature's doings. See the bee going from flower to flower with the golden pellets on her thighs, slowly and mysteriously increasing in size. If the miller were to take the toll of the grist he grinds by gathering the particles of flour from his coat and hat, as he moved rapidly about, or catching them in his pockets, he would be doing pretty nearly what the bee does. The little miller dusts herself with the pollen of the flower, and then, while on the wing, brushes it off with the fine brush on certain of her feet, and by some jugglery or other catches it in her pollen basket. One needs to look long and intently to see through the trick. Pliny says they fill their baskets with their fore feet, and that they fill their fore feet with their trunks, but it is a much more subtle operation than this. I have seen the bees come to a meal barrel in early spring, and to a pile of hardwood sawdust before there was yet anything in nature for them to work upon, and, having dusted their coats with the finer particles of the meal or the sawdust, hover on the wing above the mass till the little legerdemain feat is performed. Nature fills her baskets by the same sleight-of-hand, and the observer must be on the alert who would possess her secret. If the ancients had looked a little closer and sharper, would they ever have believed in spontaneous generation in the superficial way in which they did; that maggots, for instance, were generated spontaneously in putrid flesh? Could they not see the spawn of the blow-flies? Or, if Virgil had been a real observer of the bees, would he ever have credited, as he certainly appears to do, the fable of bees originating from the carcass of a steer? or that on windy days they carried little stones for ballast? or that two hostile swarms fought each other in the air? Indeed, the ignorance, or the false science, of the ancient observers, with regard to the whole subject of bees, is most remarkable; not false science merely with regard to their more hidden operations, but with regard to that which is open and patent to all who have eyes in their heads, and have ever had to do with them. And Pliny names authors who had devoted their whole lives to the study of the subject.

But the ancients, like women and children, were not accurate observers. Just at the critical moment their eyes were unsteady, or their fancy, or their credulity, or their impatience, got the better of them, so that their science was half fact and half fable. Thus, for instance, because the young cuckoo at times appeared to take the head of its small foster mother quite into its mouth while receiving its food, they believed that it finally devoured her. Pliny, who embodied the science of his times in his natural history, says of the wasp that it carries spiders to its nest, and then sits upon them until it hatches its young from them. A little careful observation would have shown him that this was only a half truth; that the whole truth was, that the spiders were entombed with the egg of the wasp to serve as food for the young when the egg shall have hatched.

What curious questions Plutarch discusses, as, for instance, "What is the reason that a bucket of water drawn out of a well, if it stands all night in the air that is in the well, is more cold in the morning than the rest of the water?" He could probably have given many reasons why "a watched pot never boils." The ancients, the same author says, held that the bodies of those killed by lightning never putrefy; that the sight of a ram quiets an enraged elephant; that a viper will lie stock still if touched by a beechen leaf; that a wild bull grows tame if bound with the twigs of a fig-tree; that a hen purifies herself with straw after she has laid an egg; that the deer buries his cast-off horns; that a goat stops the whole herd by holding a branch of the sea-holly in his mouth, etc. They sought to account for such things without stopping to ask, Are they true? Nature was too novel, or else too fearful, to them to be deliberately pursued and hunted down. Their youthful joy in her, or their dread and awe in her presence, may be better than our scientific satisfaction, or cool wonder, or our vague, mysterious sense of "something far more deeply interfused;" yet we cannot change with them if we would, and I, for one, would not if I could. Science does not mar nature. The railroad, Thoreau found, after all, to be about the wildest road he knew of, and the telegraph wires the best aeolian harp out of doors. Study of nature deepens the mystery and the charm because it removes the horizon farther off. We cease to fear, perhaps, but how can one cease to marvel and to love?

The fields and woods and waters about one are a book from which he may draw exhaustless entertainment, if he will. One must not only learn the writing, he must translate the language, the signs, and the hieroglyphics. It is a very quaint and elliptical writing, and much must be supplied by the wit of the translator. At any rate, the lesson is to be well conned. Gilbert White said that that locality would be found the richest in zoölogical or botanical specimens which was most thoroughly examined. For more than forty years he studied the ornithology of his district without exhausting the subject. I thought I knew my own tramping ground pretty well, but one April day, when I looked a little closer than usual into a small semi-stagnant lakelet where I had peered a hundred times before, I suddenly discovered scores of little creatures that were as new to me as so many nymphs would have been. They were partly fish-shaped, from an inch to an inch and a half long, semi-transparent, with a dark brownish line visible the entire length of them (apparently the thread upon which the life of the animal hung, and by which its all but impalpable frame was held together), and suspending themselves in the water, or impelling themselves swiftly forward by means of a double row of fine, waving, hair-like appendages, that arose from what appeared to be the back,--a kind of undulating, pappus-like wings. What was it? I did not know. None of my friends or scientific acquaintances knew. I wrote to a learned man, an authority upon fish, describing the creature as well as I could. He replied that it was only a familiar species of phyllopodous crustacean, known as Eubranchipus vernalis.

I remember that our guide in the Maine woods, seeing I had names of my own for some of the plants, would often ask me the name of this and that flower for which he had no word; and that when I could recall the full Latin term, it seemed overwhelmingly convincing and satisfying to him. It was evidently a relief to know that these obscure plants of his native heath had been found worthy of a learned name, and that the Maine woods were not so uncivil and outlandish as they might at first seem: it was a comfort to him to know that he did not live beyond the reach of botany. In like manner I found satisfaction in knowing that my novel fish had been recognized and worthily named; the title conferred a new dignity at once; but when the learned man added that it was familiarly called the "fairy shrimp," I felt a deeper pleasure. Fairy-like it certainly was, in its aerial, unsubstantial look, and in its delicate, down-like means of locomotion; but the large head, with its curious folds, and its eyes standing out in relief, as if on the heads of two pins, were gnome-like. Probably the fairy wore a mask, and wanted to appear terrible to human eyes. Then the creatures had sprung out of the earth as by magic. I found some in a furrow in a plowed field that had encroached upon a swamp. In the fall the plow had been there, and had turned up only the moist earth; now a little water was standing there, from which the April sunbeams had invoked these airy, fairy creatures. They belong to the crustaceans, but apparently no creature has so thin or impalpable a crust; you can almost see through them; certainly you can see what they have had for dinner, if they have eaten substantial food.

[Illustration: BY THE STUDY FIRE]

All we know about the private and essential natural history of the bees, the birds, the fishes, the animals, the plants, is the result of close, patient, quick-witted observation. Yet Nature will often elude one for all his pains and alertness. Thoreau, as revealed in his journal, was for years trying to settle in his own mind what was the first thing that stirred in spring, after the severe New England winter,--in what was the first sign or pulse of returning life manifest; and he never seems to have been quite sure. He could not get his salt on the tail of this bird. He dug into the swamps, he peered into the water, he felt with benumbed hands for the radical leaves of the plants under the snow; he inspected the buds on the willows, the catkins on the alders; he went out before daylight of a March morning and remained out after dark; he watched the lichens and mosses on the rocks; he listened for the birds; he was on the alert for the first frog ("Can you be absolutely sure," he says, "that you have heard the first frog that croaked in the township?"); he stuck a pin here and he stuck a pin there, and there, and still he could not satisfy himself. Nor can any one. Life appears to start in several things simultaneously. Of a warm thawy day in February the snow is suddenly covered with myriads of snow fleas looking like black, new powder just spilled there. Or you may see a winged insect in the air. On the selfsame day the grass in the spring run and the catkins on the alders will have started a little; and if you look sharply, while passing along some sheltered nook or grassy slope where the sunshine lies warm on the bare ground, you will probably see a grasshopper or two. The grass hatches out under the snow, and why should not the grasshopper? At any rate, a few such hardy specimens may be found in the latter part of our milder winters wherever the sun has uncovered a sheltered bit of grass for a few days, even after a night of ten or twelve degrees of frost. Take them in the shade, and let them freeze stiff as pokers, and when thawed out again they will hop briskly. And yet, if a poet were to put grasshoppers in his winter poem, we should require pretty full specifications of him, or else fur to clothe them with. Nature will not be cornered, yet she does many things in a corner and surreptitiously. She is all things to all men; she has whole truths, half truths, and quarter truths, if not still smaller fractions. The careful observer finds this out sooner or later. Old fox-hunters will tell you, on the evidence of their own eyes, that there is a black fox and a silver-gray fox, two species, but there are not; the black fox is black when coming toward you or running from you, and silver gray at point-blank view, when the eye penetrates the fur; each separate hair is gray the first half and black the last. This is a sample of nature's half truths.

Which are our sweet-scented wild flowers? Put your nose to every flower you pluck, and you will be surprised how your list will swell the more you smell. I plucked some wild blue violets one day, the ovata variety of the sagittata, that had a faint perfume of sweet clover, but I never could find another that had any odor. A pupil disputed with his teacher about the hepatica, claiming in opposition that it was sweet-scented. Some hepaticas are sweet-scented and some are not, and the perfume is stronger some seasons than others. After the unusually severe winter of 1880-81, the variety of hepatica called the sharp-lobed was markedly sweet in nearly every one of the hundreds of specimens I examined. A handful of them exhaled a most delicious perfume. The white ones that season were largely in the ascendant; and probably the white specimens of both varieties, one season with another, will oftenest prove sweet-scented. Darwin says a considerably larger proportion of white flowers are sweet-scented than of any other color. The only sweet violets I can depend upon are white, Viola blanda and Viola Canadensis, and white largely predominates among our other odorous wild flowers. All the fruit-trees have white or pinkish blossoms. I recall no native blue flower of New York or New England that is fragrant except in the rare case of the arrow-leaved violet, above referred to. The earliest yellow flowers, like the dandelion and yellow violets, are not fragrant. Later in the season yellow is frequently accompanied with fragrance, as in the evening primrose, the yellow lady's-slipper, horned bladderwort, and others.

My readers probably remember that on a former occasion I have mildly taken the poet Bryant to task for leading his readers to infer that the early yellow violet was sweet-scented. In view of the capriciousness of the perfume of certain of our wild flowers, I have during the past few years tried industriously to convict myself of error in respect to this flower. The round-leaved yellow violet was one of the earliest and most abundant wild flowers in the woods where my youth was passed, and whither I still make annual pilgrimages. I have pursued it on mountains and in lowlands, in "beechen woods" and amid the hemlocks; and while, with respect to its earliness, it overtakes the hepatica in the latter part of April, as do also the dog's-tooth violet and the claytonia, yet the first hepaticas, where the two plants grow side by side, bloom about a week before the first violet. And I have yet to find one that has an odor that could be called a perfume. A handful of them, indeed, has a faint, bitterish smell, not unlike that of the dandelion in quality; but if every flower that has a smell is sweet-scented, then every bird that makes a noise is a songster.

On the occasion above referred to, I also dissented from Lowell's statement, in "Al Fresco," that in early summer the dandelion blooms, in general, with the buttercup and the clover. I am aware that such criticism of the poets is small game, and not worth the powder. General truth, and not specific fact, is what we are to expect of the poets. Bryant's "Yellow Violet" poem is tender and appropriate, and such as only a real lover and observer of nature could feel or express; and Lowell's "Al Fresco" is full of the luxurious feeling of early summer, and this is, of course, the main thing; a good reader cares for little else; I care for little else myself. But when you take your coin to the assay office it must be weighed and tested, and in the comments referred to I (unwisely perhaps) sought to smelt this gold of the poets in the naturalist's pot, to see what alloy of error I could detect in it. Were the poems true to their last word? They were not, and much subsequent investigation has only confirmed my first analysis. The general truth is on my side, and the specific fact, if such exists in this case, on the side of the poets. It is possible that there may be a fragrant yellow violet, as an exceptional occurrence, like that of the sweet-scented, arrow-leaved species above referred to, and that in some locality it may have bloomed before the hepatica; also that Lowell may have seen a belated dandelion or two in June, amid the clover and the buttercups; but, if so, they were the exception, and not the rule,--the specific or accidental fact, and not the general truth.

Dogmatism about nature, or about anything else, very often turns out to be an ungrateful cur that bites the hand that reared it. I speak from experience. I was once quite certain that the honey-bee did not work upon the blossoms of the trailing arbutus, but while walking in the woods one April day I came upon a spot of arbutus swarming with honey-bees. They were so eager for it that they crawled under the leaves and the moss to get at the blossoms, and refused on the instant the hive-honey which I happened to have with me, and which I offered them. I had had this flower under observation more than twenty years, and had never before seen it visited by honey-bees. The same season I saw them for the first time working upon the flower of bloodroot and of adder's-tongue. Hence I would not undertake to say again what flowers bees do not work upon. Virgil implies that they work upon the violet, and for aught I know they may. I have seen them very busy on the blossoms of the white oak, though this is not considered a honey or pollen yielding tree. From the smooth sumac they reap a harvest in midsummer, and in March they get a good grist of pollen from the skunk-cabbage.

I presume, however, it would be safe to say that there is a species of smilax with an unsavory name that the bee does not visit, herbacea. The production of this plant is a curious freak of nature. I find it growing along the fences where one would look for wild roses or the sweetbrier; its recurving or climbing stem, its glossy, deep-green, heart-shaped leaves, its clustering umbels of small greenish-yellow flowers, making it very pleasing to the eye; but to examine it closely one must positively hold his nose. It would be too cruel a joke to offer it to any person not acquainted with it to smell. It is like the vent of a charnel-house. It is first cousin to the trilliums, among the prettiest of our native wild flowers, and the same bad blood crops out in the purple trillium or birthroot.

Nature will include the disagreeable and repulsive also. I have seen the phallic fungus growing in June under a rosebush. There was the rose, and beneath it, springing from the same mould, was this diabolical offering to Priapus. With the perfume of the roses into the open window came the stench of this hideous parody, as if in mockery. I removed it, and another appeared in the same place shortly afterward. The earthman was rampant and insulting. Pan is not dead yet. At least he still makes a ghastly sign here and there in nature.

The good observer of nature exists in fragments, a trait here and a trait there. Each person sees what it concerns him to see. The fox-hunter knows pretty well the ways and habits of the fox, but on any other subject he is apt to mislead you. He comes to see only fox traits in whatever he looks upon. The bee-hunter will follow the bee, but lose the bird. The farmer notes what affects his crops and his earnings, and little else. Common people, St. Pierre says, observe without reasoning, and the learned reason without observing. If one could apply to the observation of nature the sense and skill of the South American rastreador, or trailer, how much he would track home! This man's eye, according to the accounts of travelers, is keener than a hound's scent. A fugitive can no more elude him than he can elude fate. His perceptions are said to be so keen that the displacement of a leaf or pebble, or the bending down of a spear of grass, or the removal of a little dust from the fence are enough to give him the clew. He sees the half-obliterated footprints of a thief in the sand, and carries the impression in his eye till a year afterward, when he again detects the same footprint in the suburbs of a city, and the culprit is tracked home and caught. I knew a man blind from his youth who not only went about his own neighborhood without a guide, turning up to his neighbor's gate or door as unerringly as if he had the best of eyes, but who would go many miles on an errand to a new part of the country. He seemed to carry a map of the township in the bottom of his feet, a most minute and accurate survey. He never took the wrong road, and he knew the right house when he had reached it. He was a miller and fuller, and ran his mill at night while his sons ran it by day. He never made a mistake with his customers' bags or wool, knowing each man's by the sense of touch. He frightened a colored man whom he detected stealing, as if he had seen out of the back of his head. Such facts show one how delicate and sensitive a man's relation to outward nature through his bodily senses may become. Heighten it a little more, and he could forecast the weather and the seasons, and detect hidden springs and minerals. A good observer has something of this delicacy and quickness of perception. All the great poets and naturalists have it. Agassiz traces the glaciers like a rastreador; and Darwin misses no step that the slow but tireless gods of physical change have taken, no matter how they cross or retrace their course. In the obscure fish-worm he sees an agent that has kneaded and leavened the soil like giant hands.

One secret of success in observing nature is capacity to take a hint; a hair may show where a lion is hid. One must put this and that together, and value bits and shreds. Much alloy exists with the truth. The gold of nature does not look like gold at the first glance. It must be smelted and refined in the mind of the observer. And one must crush mountains of quartz and wash hills of sand to get it. To know the indications is the main matter. People who do not know the secret are eager to take a walk with the observer to find where the mine is that contains such nuggets, little knowing that his ore-bed is but a gravel-heap to them. How insignificant appear most of the facts which one sees in his walks, in the life of the birds, the flowers, the animals, or in the phases of the landscape, or the look of the sky!--insignificant until they are put through some mental or emotional process and their true value appears. The diamond looks like a pebble until it is cut. One goes to Nature only for hints and half truths. Her facts are crude until you have absorbed them or translated them. Then the ideal steals in and lends a charm in spite of one. It is not so much what we see as what the thing seen suggests. We all see about the same; to one it means much, to another little. A fact that has passed through the mind of man, like lime or iron that has passed through his blood, has some quality or property superadded or brought out that it did not possess before. You may go to the fields and the woods, and gather fruit that is ripe for the palate without any aid of yours, but you cannot do this in science or in art. Here truth must be disentangled and interpreted,--must be made in the image of man. Hence all good observation is more or less a refining and transmuting process, and the secret is to know the crude material when you see it. I think of Wordsworth's lines:--

"The mighty world Of eye and ear, both what they half create and what perceive;"which is as true in the case of the naturalist as of the poet; both "half create" the world they describe. Darwin does something to his facts as well as Tennyson to his. Before a fact can become poetry, it must pass through the heart or the imagination of the poet; before it can become science, it must pass through the understanding of the scientist. Or one may say, it is with the thoughts and half thoughts that the walker gathers in the woods and fields, as with the common weeds and coarser wild flowers which he plucks for a bouquet,--wild carrot, purple aster, moth mullein, sedge, grass, etc.: they look common and uninteresting enough there in the fields, but the moment he separates them from the tangled mass, and brings them indoors, and places them in a vase, say of some choice glass, amid artificial things,--behold, how beautiful! They have an added charm and significance at once; they are defined and identified, and what was common and familiar becomes unexpectedly attractive. The writer's style, the quality of mind he brings, is the vase in which his commonplace impressions and incidents are made to appear so beautiful and significant.

Man can have but one interest in nature, namely, to see himself reflected or interpreted there; and we quickly neglect both poet and philosopher who fail to satisfy, in some measure, this feeling.

###

www.ingramcontent.com/pod-product-compliance
Lightning Source LLC
Chambersburg PA
CBHW062018280526
45787CB00005B/2148